The Official "How To Man-Up" Book

By
Michael Scott Parrish

"The world is a dangerous place, not because of those who do evil, but because of those who look on and do nothing."

Albert Einstein

Chapter's

"A quitter never wins and a winner never quits"

Napoleon Hill

DEDICATION

In November of 2010, the hottest election race in the country was the one for the United States Senate seat which Democratic Senate Majority Leader Harry Reid of Nevada had held for the past thirty years. He was facing a tough, resourceful, conservative challenger: Sharon Angle. This race was of special importance to me and my family. Harry Reid was the senator who so loudly proclaimed, to the entire world, "The war is lost!" Those comments are without a doubt the most unconscionable remarks ever spoken by a public official while a country was at war. This pathetic example of a leader said these words, not during a truce or during some form of peace accord, but while our brave and committed soldiers were actually still fighting for America.

It sickened me, and many others as well, and I truly believe that it was a treasonous act and that he should have immediately resigned or have been forced out of office. But, as so often happens, the prescribed answer was to be an insincere and scripted apology, citing his remorse for making the statement, and his excuses about the misunderstanding to the American people was to suffice. This was a disgusting slap across the face to all American's and it was severely undermining to our military and Americas morale.

And even though I was a child, I can also remember, and can still see, the disturbing images of Jane Fonda, proudly sitting atop a machine gun turret of the North Viet Cong, while laughing and smiling into the camera as American soldiers were being killed and crippled fighting for this traitor's freedom. Those images haunt me with a stinging sensation, and the points of comparison between these two vermin line up perfectly. It baffles the mind why they are allowed to live in this country.

Not long ago, Larry Parrish…my first cousin, who was dearly loved by all of our family and friends…was tragically killed in action in a roadside bomb explosion, perpetrated by terrorists, while serving heroically in Iraq. He fought and died for all Americans, and Harry Reid has the audacity and cowardice to proclaim that "the war is lost." The only thing that was lost, Harry, was your ability to be a man. Our military certainly hasn't lost anything, and my cousin Larry Parrish was more of a man than you could ever possibly fathom. You have absolutely no idea what it means to man-up.

Consider yourself a very lucky man, Mr. Reid, because if his father…my uncle Bob Parrish, were alive when you made such a statement, he would have shown you exactly what kind of boxer you really were and that you are not what you have proclaimed yourself to be.

Sharon Angle, we are indebted to you for your truthful words as you so beautifully and eloquently challenged Harry Reid, in a national television debate, to "man-up" and apologize to the American people. My wife and I wept tears of joy as we watched you crush this timid and befuddled man into retreating as fast he could. run. And we are sorry that Nevada re-elected a man of such a pedigree.

There are no words that can ever describe the satisfaction as we watched you doing this. This man is a coward and does not deserve to be treated as anything other than what he is.

2010 also marked the passing of my wife's father, James Cunningham. Due to events beyond my control, and with great sorrow, I was unable to attend his funeral and the accompanying military ceremony, which I had so desperately wanted to witness. I am still remorseful and somewhat ashamed that I was not able to attend. There are reasons for this; however, I accept full responsibility for not being present at the service and now offer this message, and the accompanying eulogy, which I had written and was read at the ceremony, at the request of my wife to her father.

It is my gesture to his memory of my endearing sorrow, gratitude and respect for his life.

"If you can imagine it, you can achieve it; if you can dream it, you can become it."

William Arthur Ward

"THE MEASURE OF A MAN"

Dearest friends and family. It is with deep regret and heartfelt remorse that I must now address you in absence. It was with my complete desire and tried attempt to attend this ceremony personally along with my wife and our children. Unfortunately, the task proved difficult and ultimately impossible for all of us to attend. I can now only offer this eulogy as a written tribute to my wife's father James Cunningham as she has requested me to speak for her in memory to her father. A man whom I will always remember with the utmost respect and admiration.

I met Jim Cunningham twenty two years ago in 1988. I instantly realized that my future wife's father was not a man who treaded lightly or his personal beliefs and opinions were dictated to be politically correct. Imagine that! A man who actually spoke his mind and wasn't afraid to say it. Anyone who has ever met Dad can testify to that and knows exactly what I mean. Simply put he was a "man's-man and old school to the bone."

He never pretended to be anything other than who he was and I am still and always be in awe of his bravery and dedication to his family, friends and his devotion and service to our country for which he pledged his very life on numerous occasions during his service in World War II.

Over the next several years, I persistently asked Dad to divulge the details of his exploits and service during the war, only to be refused and told by my wife to stop asking her father these questions, because he would not discuss those events and would not speak of them. Ever.

However; I wanted to know and thought that it was paramount and very important to preserve the history for our children because of the significant importance and the sacrifice he had made for our country. So, finally, after visiting our family for a week at our home in Las Vegas Nevada on his way to a Veterans war re-union in Reno, and at the ripe old age of 80…and a bottle of Crown Royal. I once again asked Dad to tell me and to reveal the details of the war. But this time, and in true Jim Cunningham Irish fashion he looked me directly in the eyes and said in a loud and thunderous voice "Alright, damn it, I am going to tell you once and that's it!"

For the next hour or so he recited what had happened and I wrote down every word. He spoke in direct and in simple terms and without hesitation and with humble humility. He did not brag nor boast. His memory was precise and detailed and I shall never forget as long as I live. Some of the fighting was house to house, room to room and was ultimately, hand to hand combat.

The intensity of his eyes were that of a man who had been to the edge of hell and lived to tell about it. He was a decorated war hero (Two Bronze Star's with Oak leaf Cluster) who gave sincere homage to all of his fellow soldiers who he had fought with and to the ones who had died beside him for the price of freedom in the black darkness of tyranny.

Looking back now I can fully and better understand as I see the exact same fearless and determined look as I look into the deep green eyes of my beautiful wife whenever she is rallied for a fight. Which I must say is not a place where you ever want to be! She too simply does not know how to quit or give up. I wonder where she got that from? As a child my wife has confided in me that she did not understand why her father was often mad and quick to respond to many situations with anger. She has said now she understands.

Perhaps now we all know why and the cost that was willingly paid by this brave and courageous American. A loving father who did his best for his family, friends and country.

Six months ago we visited Dad and talked about the every day events of our children family and the state of our country. He spoke of his immense pride of his son's and grandchildren and their accomplishments. He was also disgusted and sickened with the weak and apologetic attitude that our nation was taking against a deadly enemy that had dared to threaten the safety of his children and grandchildren he had so fiercely fought and protected his entire life. He said shaking his head, "I just don't know if it was worth it." Instantly, I watched their eyes meet as Shelly Jo looked a her father directly and boldly stated with the utmost determination as she replied, "Oh, Yes it was Dad." He smiled and gleamed at her and simply said "Ok."

Words cannot express the quiet confidence and comfort that I feel in solace knowing that the same blood that courses through my wife and our precious children's veins is the same blood as James Cunningham.

"We shall see you on the other side"
With all our love Your loving daughter, son-in-law and grandchildren.

This book is also empirically dedicated to my beautiful and loving wife, Shelly Jo Cunningham Parrish, one of the strongest women I have ever known. She is the defining instrument that has compelled me to write this book. She has told me for years that I should, and instinctively knew that whenever I was weak, hesitant or felt that I could not continue with whatever conflict I was facing, that she would instantly command me to "man-up" and she meant it. She started saying this to me many years ago, and long, long before this term had become fashionable, and she still does. She was the first person I heard use the term, and I believe she may have coined it.

Her strength was evident from the moment I first met her, and her father was probably her greatest influence. She is a magnificent and beautiful woman who, though not as vocal or verbal as I am, when she is cornered, I feel a great sadness for any adversary who wishes to challenge her, male or female.

The next dedication is to my mother and father for always insisting that I be myself and teaching me all of my moral and patriotic beliefs. You are both dearly loved. I could not have done this without you.

I further dedicate this work to my uncle, Tom Parrish, for his unwavering belief and confidence in me and for his strength, responsibility and undeniable intelligence. Thank you for showing me what "Two hundred pounds of determined man can do!" He is a real man's man and is an excellent male role model, which all men of substance and character should try to emulate. He is my hero.

Next, to the wonderful women in my life and for the foundation that they instilled in me. My grandma June, great-grandma Evie, all of my aunt's and most affectionately, my third grade teacher, Mrs. Peavey, who had taught me more in the third grade than all my other years in school combined. I have been very lucky to have had all of these wonderful women in my life.

Finally, to my grandma Parrish, Ethel Marie, who raised eleven children practically by herself and without fear. This includes surviving the Great Depression. She was a person who had innate wisdom and supernatural qualities, that are only describable if you had actually known her, including healing powers. She was of Scot-Irish and Cherokee descent and was completely comfortable and at ease in her natural place in life. I have never since met anyone like her, other than my wife…who is actually freakishly similar in spirit and natural appearance.

It seems almost unbelievable, but she instinctively knew and described so vividly to me, at a very young and impressionable age…the vast mysteries and exact philosophy of many of today's most respected and admired teachers. I'm talking about today's modern life coaches, philosophers, doctors and professors who have made their careers out of sharing with the world their keen insight and wisdom. Decades before they had become known to the world, she just knew it, and it made an unforgettable impression.

Please believe me when I say that she knew how to "man-up" like no one I have ever seen! She has been gone for over thirty years and I am still mourning her. "You were right, Grandma, I can do anything if I believe that I can."

"My Indian Angel Above"

"THE OFFICIAL HOW TO MAN-UP BOOK"

INTRODUCTION

"The Official How to Man-Up" book and show are a philosophy and an effort that celebrates all the things about being a man. They cover good and bad subjects alike, but with a special emphasis for men to "Man Up" and to take charge of their lives, and why it is time for men to take full responsibility for their actions, and meet those conflicts head-on, aggressively, by taking control and defining themselves as men.

It is a call for men to realize that we are under attack, and it is a real threat that needs to be both acknowledged and addressed. Not in the sense that we are being attacked physically, but rather, that our image and the natural order are under fire and why we are in need of leaders. The book and show are meant to explore exactly what is happening and why.

We will adamantly acknowledge and encourage men to become more than themselves and to summon the courage and strength to set an overwhelming and powerful example to everyone of exactly what it means and how to act like a man. We shall show real examples of inspiring and great men of the past, present, and future, and the awe-inspiring accomplishments they have made and their sacrifices.

We will also expose the men who have lost their nerve and failed or simply given up, and why they have done it.

Where have the historically iconic alpha-male defining role models of the past all gone? It appears that Hollywood has especially portrayed us to be submissive, overly apologetic and weak and that they encourage this image. Is this the message we want to send to our children and our enemies?

By nature we are not weak, submissive or apologetic. We are tigers, and we deserve to be treated with the respect due to such a creature; otherwise, those who don't should be willing to pay the price for pulling on our tails. I find it very funny that when this actually does happen and a "tiger" is ready for a fight, the media is shocked by our behavior, for revealing our true nature. This kind of constant schoolgirl gossip-commentary by the liberal media is ridiculously silly and virtually endless.

I call this the "Feminization of Hollywood," and we are going to expose these weaklings for what they really are, by showing examples of how they are desperately trying to change the true image of man.

I only ask that you decide if it's not true and judge it for yourself. Isn't it time we stopped pussy-footing around and waiting for someone to attack us? My father always told me that being a target is not a very good impression to give someone, and I for one refuse to continue to be bombarded by others who insist on portraying men as they see fit. I also refuse to continue to stand for us being mindlessly led by the hand, as if we were timid children, into apologizing constantly for our actions, regardless of the event or situation.

Why are men being publicly humiliated for the personal actions that have occurred in their private lives, and why are they constantly persecuted if they don't seem to be truly sincere enough in their apologies and don't give in to the media's requests? Most of the time, it's none of their business and they should be told such.

What would John Wayne or Frank Sinatra have done if confronted or cornered by today's liberal media for some trivial personal event or family tragedy?

Can you imagine those guys being prodded by Gloria Allred into meekly apologizing for their smoking, drinking, or their desire and attraction to beautiful women? What do you think their response would have been? Exactly.

We all know what would have happened. What has happened? Did our balls suddenly fall off? Where are all of the strong male leaders? These questions are answered in the book and will be topics of discussion in the supporting show.

However, our prime intention and goal is that men always realize their mistakes and do the honorable, just and right thing, whatever that may be. But it must be on their own terms. That's the mettle of what men of substance and character do. To "Man Up" and show the world who they are and why.

Thus, our mission and goal is to energize men to look into their hearts, minds, and souls and to realize our natural evolution and history in becoming men and to be proud of who and what we are.

I also want men to be able to read the book and to become inspired to go out and Man-Up whenever necessary. Our future and our survival truly depend on it. There is nothing that tastes as sour as regret.

"Many of us have indeed become lost, but don't worry because, we are going to get it all back!" Because, it's time to "Man Up."

"Twenty years from now you will be more disappointed by the things that you didn't do than by the ones you did do. So throw off the bowlines. Sail away from the safe harbor. Catch the trade winds in your sails. Explore. Dream. Discover"

Mark Twain

CHAPTER 1

THE REASON

I am deeply honored and thankful that you have taken the time to read this book…it is my first! I am grateful and optimistically hopeful that you will understand it and that you will be able to decide for yourself if I am telling the truth and that once you do, you will use your new powers and will be able to demonstrate them to others as well. I have filled this book with my thoughts, stories, and historically-related quotes from some of the greatest men that have ever lived; and from some that I have personally known. This book contains their incredible related wisdom that is astonishingly similar and it is all relevant to each of my steps and the stories.

Why are these quotes from history so strikingly similar? It will be very easy for you to decide that on your own. Because, as you will see these are real and symbolic examples of men who have manned-up throughout history. They are important events that have been carved into our history These men are our ancient brothers and warriors who made these statements for a reason. And so, I have written and compiled the associated stories and the man-up philosophy to encourage you and to show you the true and factual meaning of my findings and obvious comparisons and the importance of my observations and the consequences we are facing in today's modern climate if things continue as they have been.

Now: how am I qualified for such a task, you ask? Well, first of all, I shoot from the hip and tell it like I see it. I have absolutely no formal training when it comes to writing a book and I also don't give a damn, whether or not I am politically correct, or sensitive enough for my readers, because I am not trying out for some kind of popularity contest. I am here to man-up, and to help others to man-up.

The truth is, I was suspended from school several times, and barely made it through high school. I failed almost every English and history class I had ever taken, and I remember very little of anything that I ever learned in any of those classes. And I'm not a professional writer. I am not a doctor, nor do I possess any other type of award or accolade that has ever been printed, as a certificate of distinction, on a fancy piece of paper in relation to this field of study. I am not claiming to be an educated expert on the subject, nor do I wish to have such credentials.

But I do know this: I know who men are. Because I am a man, and I know exactly what men think. And I know what men are supposed to do and what men need to do, and what they aren't supposed to do. So I think that more than qualifies me on the subject. "Go big or go home!" that is what I believe, and it has always served me well. I also have a deep devotion to our country, I love America.

When I started writing this book, the words literally flew onto the pages, and I wrote the entire book in a matter of days. That's how easily it came to me, no effort or struggle at all.

My copy editor, who by the way, is my 15 year old daughter Michaela, "Katie Jo" Parrish…well, that's another story altogether. You see I typically like to use a lot of profanity and I always have. Ever since I was hustling pool for dime's at the Belton, Missouri pool hall (Glen's Recreation) when I was 9 year's old. But, using the F-bomb isn't going to help me win this war so I have refrained from my usual verbal descriptions.

Also my Dad told me not to do it, and I don't mess with the old man. I also decided that I have no intention of waiting around for someone else's approval, such as a publisher, to give me permission to go ahead and print my book. I will do it by myself, without help or influence from anyone else, and I like it that way. We shall see who is interested and what happens.

My life long, and one of my dearest friend's Seth Gortenberg in Kansas City, Missouri has always shown me that this is how a real mans true strength is measured, and he has always forged his own way, with little help and I have always admired him and his keen wit and superior fearless attitude. His older brother Michael Gortenberg is also the same caliber of man. They both are very powerful, successful and smart. Seth has counseled me and has helped me enormously throughout my career and has never questioned my ability. He is without a doubt one of the most, if not the most capable, intelligent and absolutely brilliant men I have ever known. He is cut from a different kind of cloth. Dix Wellington from my hometown is also a lifelong friend and I consider him to be of this valiant tribe and a brother as well.

One of my favorite historical quotes, and a source of tremendous associated meaning in relationship with my subject and serves as an excellent example.

When the legions of Rome landed on the beaches in what is now known as England, they were severely outnumbered and were a great distance from their homes and supplies. They did not know just what was lying in store for them; perhaps death and crushing defeat, and to never return home to their families and loved ones. Their general had decided on a plan, one that would make it very clear to his legions of men, all of whom adored him by the way, exactly what their future was going to be, regardless of what happened to them, and in a very masterful and committed fashion. Upon landing the ships, the fearless commander ordered his troops to the very top of the mighty cliffs of Dover, overlooking the ocean, and as the men stood high atop this mighty precipice and gazed back down, their eyes were met with the startling realization of the absolute resolve and unwavering commitment of the general. He heroically proclaimed,

"Now, burn the ships."   *Julius Caesar*

The soldiers knew, right then and there, that there was not going to be any retreat, and that the only options were victory or death. I also consider myself to be on a combat mission, and I don't believe in taking any prisoners. "I'm in   the kicking-some-ass, writing-a-book business, and brother....business is gonna be-a-booming!"

You see, there is little doubt that I am on to something. It seems that everyone wants to man-up! Even the good folks at Miller Beer know that it's time to man-up. I see it everywhere. So, perhaps I should warn you what you all are in for in the upcoming pages. I don't play defense. I play offense only, and I do it vigorously. However, If I did play defense, I would aspire to be a Jack Lambert, Mike Curtis, Willie Lanier, or of course the mighty Dick Butkus. Oh yeah, that's right. Those guys define the words "old school."

Did you ever see the video clip of the idiot fan who ran out onto the field, when the Baltimore Colts were playing, and middle linebacker Mike "The animal" Curtis is seen menacingly watching this drunken fool as he tries to steal the football? Then, he suddenly and violently body- slams the guy into the ground like a grade school bully? If that were to happen today, Curtis would be expelled from the league, fined, arrested by the police, charged with assault and battery, and sued for millions. All of this would inevitably happen, fueled by a very long line of ecstatically excited, but heartfelt and concerned lawyers who would loudly proclaim that this poor fellow's rights were violated on national TV.

However, those same champions of justice would have absolutely no compassion, feeling or regard for the rights of the players on the field, the fans, or what was at stake as the "victim" successfully interrupted and destroyed the moment and flow of the game that was taking place, and the importance and meaning of it to the millions of people who were a part of it. The lawyers would complain loudly about the rights of the "poor victim" instead of honestly calling it what it really was and what everyone watching knows to be true, which was that this guy was acting like a total drunken jackass and got exactly what he deserved! Money seems to be able to conveniently distort the truth for these masterful wordsmiths as they see fit. Bill Clinton especially, and his wife.

Note: (except for my attorney Matthew Callister, of Las Vegas, Nevada, who is a true peoples champion and a legal genius!)

It's pathetic, but true. Football was better before it became big business and the quarterbacks started sliding into second base. Bradshaw never did. I also like my rock and roll the same way as I like my football. Vintage Ted Nugent, AC/DC and Van Halen really loud, and full blast!

Although; I say that with some reservations when it comes to Ted Nugent, because; I am from Kansas City, Missouri (home of the greatest rock fans in the world) and in the late 70s, "The Nuge" once performed a sold out concert at "Arrowhead Stadium" where he played so unbelievably loud it was reported that he was heard as far away as Blue Springs, Missouri, which is about 20 miles away. He rocked so hard, that he literally shook the earth! He was and still is dearly loved by thousands of fans in my hometown and I am the one standing at the front of the line.

Mr. Nugent is a vetted elder of the tribe of rock and roll, and even now as a man in his 60s, he can still "crush, kill and destroy" anything in his path. And not just musically either, I personally think he should run for office. He has become very political in recent years and I once saw him on a show where he was pitted against famed attorney Gloria Allred and his mind was so blazingly fast he completely dominated her in the interview. He replied in a very heated exchange against this liberal champion... *"You tell me. You're the lawyer!"*

Even Allred was very impressed…and she laughed at the exchange, it was that good. And if you haven't read any of his books, ("**Ted, White and Blue**", my personal favorite) do yourself a favor and pick up a copy, because, "The Motor City Madman" is sharper than the buck-knife that he uses for skinning the countless carcasses he kills and then feeds his family with on a yearly basis. He is also very tuned in to the world. I respect his fortitude and his uncompromising attitude, when it comes to his gun's and hunting agenda. I also admire his passion, commitment and his determination for America. It is very refreshing to be able to know exactly where a man stands and with Ted Nugent, there is zero room for the mincing of words. He, is this book… in spades!

I do know this, if America was ever invaded by vicious flesh eating alien's, the North Koreans, or if genetically engineered T-Rex dinosaurs' ever came back to life and were eating everyone in sight…I would want me and my family to be as close to "Ted's" place as possible.

Because, whoever the poor dumb bastards were, that would ever be foolish enough to try an act of such supreme stupidity, would surly be met with a lethal barrage of carnage, death, and destruction of such epic and biblical proportion's that God himself would probably proclaim, "man-down Ted, man-down!" But, the BBQ would certainly be friggin awesome!

I have been asked by several of my friends and family: why I am so passionate in regard to this book? Well, first of all, I believe in what I am doing and believe that everything I have said is true. I don't expect everyone to agree with me, but as I have said, I don't really care and have no intention of trying to change everyone else's mind or opinion.

Especially those weak men who cannot see it right in front of their eyes and who refuse my help. I am, however, convinced that what I am talking about is true; that I know what I'm talking about and that I can prove it. Anyone with a brain can see what's going on, and what is happening to our society as men. The role that we have in the world is changing, and not for the better.

Perhaps you think that this is some kind of a joke; I can assure you that it is not. I am a man, I am deeply concerned, and I feel that I must act. It's pretty simple, really, but I am shocked to realize that there are many men who have simply decided to go along with the norm and not rock the boat. Kind of like robots that have been programmed to do so. To me this kind of timid behavior is brittle and unnatural.

And that is exactly what is happening, and now is the time to do something about it. I am here to tell you, as a full grown man, that I am ready to show the world that I am willing to take a stand and I am not going to surrender, ever. I am the proud father of five sons and two daughters that depend on me and their mother to teach them and guide them into life as adults. We welcome that challenge and are very privileged to have been parents. It is not surprising, though, that women seem to know instinctively and clearly what they want in a man, and they know exactly what a man is and what isn't. They also aren't afraid to tell you, either, if you ask them. And I have.

One clear message is that everyone knows the term "Man-Up" and they also have an opinion about it. I, on the other hand, have written a book to help to better illuminate the situation, and to ignite a no-holds barred firestorm on the subject. So "Bring it!"

If you don't think that this is really happening and you want to challenge me then...let's get busy. I hope that you do, so all of the rest of us men and women who aren't totally whipped and crazy can easily identify you and we will know exactly who you are. (The movie **"Inglorious Bastards"** was identical in it's approval of uniforms for identifying Nazis.) and I personally encourage you to do so and to man up.

I should warn you though, if you are not mentally prepared to go "toe to toe" and explain exactly why you think that all of this is not really happening you should probably reconsider.

Because, I am very serious about this and I welcome the opportunity to show you, who, what, and most importantly why. Also here is a shout-out to all of our many friends and family, across the entire country, especially to everyone back home in Missouri. We love all of you and we are very grateful for your overwhelming support.

However, we already know and are aware of your one-of-a-kind, go-get-em attitude and the rock solid kind of people all of you are. Men, women, boys, girls, grandmas, grandpas, we salute you and we shall do this together!

Are you with me and are you ready? Outstanding. Now, "**Burn The Ships**" and get ready to Man Up, like never before!

"The men who have succeeded are the ones who have chosen one line and stuck to it."

Andrew Carnegie

"Brave Heart"
(My all-time favorite personal quote)

Aye, fight and you may die. Run, and you'll live... at least a while. And dying in your beds, many years from now, would you be willing' to trade ALL the days, from this day to that, for one chance, just one chance, to come back here and tell our enemies that they may take our lives, but they'll never take... OUR FREEDOM!

Alba gu bràth!
"Scotland forever!"   *William Wallace*

Always bear in mind that your own resolution to succeed is more important than any other.

Abraham Lincoln

CHAPTER 2:

TAKE ACTION

Why is it time to "Man-Up" and take action? Read this book and you can decide for yourself if I am right about the time being now. Where would we be today if men hadn't taken action at key points in history and decided to kick ass?

Would America still exist, or would we all be speaking Japanese? That was Japan's mission and their sworn oath as they ruthlessly sneak-attacked and killed thousands of Americans at Pearl Harbor…to either destroy the United States or to enslave us.

Even after such a cowardly and sinister attack on us, a few years later they were hospitably given the opportunity to surrender. Was this how they treated America? Were their actions against us and the war atrocities that they committed against America and others so generous? Not hardly. They committed unspeakable acts against the citizens of the Philippines, and if they had invaded America, it would have been the same thing: it was their sworn blood oath to kill everyone. Japan decided to continue to fight on after this fateful warning and defiantly continued on trying to kill all of us, only to be annihilated by an overwhelming weapon of mass destruction, of biblical proportions. An act which could have been avoided, they had been forewarned. They did finally surrender, but only after we were forced to use this terrible weapon…twice!

They soon understood America's superior power and resolve. Tragic and sad, but also true. Where would we be today if our courageous warriors of "The Greatest Generation" had decided not to storm the beaches in Normandy, France, on D-Day, or if they'd felt that Adolph Hitler really wasn't a mass-murdering maniac that needed to be destroyed? Perhaps he was just misunderstood.

Or, what if they'd decided to just talk nice to the Third Reich and negotiate, similar to what our current leader, President Barrack Obama, has suggested we do with Al-Quida? It is almost certain that we would all be speaking German right now if they hadn't taken action during World War II.

It takes action and courage to accomplish the impossible. The timid and weak never succeed as champions. Most of the time, they only serve as lessons to the strong on how not to act and what not to do. Men have always been in situations that require action if they are to be victorious. We have always been challenged into fighting for our survival and our right to exist, typically by other men who have taken a hostile action towards us. Wars, religion, acts of nature, plagues and most commonly, the affection (or lack thereof) of a woman. Yes, we men love to fight over nookie!

There have been more wars and battles fought over women than we can count and there will be many more. Throughout the history of our planet we have battled each other and killed one another for some reason or other, but one thing is for certain, men have always taken action to win the day.

Today, it seems that men are being victimized by numerous enemies. Specifically, the liberal media and Hollywood lead this attack. The iconic image and history of the strong male role model is obviously under attack. Look at how the leading man of the past is often portrayed in today's modern commercials, television and movies.

How many times have you seen the leader of the family become submissive in his role as the head of the household, and the obvious (usually feminine) weaker male seen as the stronger, wittier, smarter man that everyone wishes they were? What a bunch of bull crap. Not that this has never happened, it's just not the way it usually does.

There are forces out there that are actually trying to re-write the natural order of things and to disguise the true way of things by changing history through the media. Usually this is done by implementing some form of bizarre political correctness, which has already been proven to kill innocent Americans. All because someone didn't have the balls to take action and do something.

"Political Correctness doesn't change us, it shuts us up!"

Glenn Beck

Ft. Hood, Texas is a textbook example. There were countless reports of this terrorist-in-the- making, and frightening examples of his distorted behavior, long before his murderous rampage. Still, no one did anything because of the fear of being called a racist or being found guilty of not being politically correct and sensitive enough to Muslims' rights.

You tell me: is it worse to be accused of a despicable act, or to allow one to happen when it could have easily been stopped before thirteen innocent people were murdered? I can only imagine the sorrow in the hearts of our military personnel at Ft. Hood that knew about this coward and did nothing to prevent it.

Why did it have to happen? Because the media has demonized anyone who stands up and says a defiant no! Not on my watch! And even if they do, they are accused, tried and convicted instantly by the media and hounded to the ends of the earth by Gloria Allred or that other jack-ass Keith Olberman.

Jesus, she is a friggin' one-woman army, a super-liberal terminator who apparently never sleeps, because I see her constantly.

Whenever someone has been busted for something, she is always there to champion the other party. Illegal aliens, child molesters, murderers, you name it, she loves them all and she is pissed!

She must have her ear glued to the police scanner because she is always in the picture. I guess that they couldn't find Bill O'Reilly's phone number to represent her kind of "journalism."

The obvious motive for this is to make everyone the same. Men and women, boys and girls alike, everyone. Just one great big giant world of equality and love. History has shown that males and females, boys and girls, are not the same. We are different, and the media's only chance to fool and push their agenda to the public. They try to change reality by their propagandist agenda in movies and TV, and by visual brainwashing with lies.

The good news is that the media's (especially TV and movies) days of running rampant are almost over. The media is consuming itself like a flesh-eating bacteria. Mainly because TV and movie executives and programmers really have no idea what American audiences want or what the hell they are doing. An excellent example of this would be the reality shows. Anything and everything, twisted and distorted for all of America to see unfold. Their carnival barkers flaunting and exploiting people to the less fortunate, uneducated and socially lost and amoral, while the shows' producers profit from their exploitation, angst and pain. Usually there is nothing real about any of it. Most is all staged and looks fake. Game show contest true love? This is so stupid and the prize, which is marriage, is pathetically ridiculous and is slated for failure.

TV now also runs commercials…most of which a college graduate cannot even understand, while the featured program is running and during other commercials. Yes, commercials in other commercials and during the featured program.

Another example would be the creation and success of cartoons for adults. This is simply astonishing to me. I cannot believe that anyone would ever watch these shows, yet there are too many to count and more all the time. Why? Obviously, because TV has lost its creativity and cannot come up with anything new and interesting. Television, for years now, has dumbed down programming and tried to brainwash our youth. The internet will overtake television, and it's already happening, but I'm sorry to say that some of it is actually working. Our young people are watching these shows and many think that these examples are real, and that this is normal behavior.

Most are lies, and the perpetrators need to be put on notice. Why are there constant images of the once-powerful righteous leading man being weak and feminine? Do history and real life events support such a description? No, they don't.

However, they do if the man or culture has been wiped out and killed. Survival is accomplished by defeating the opposing force; by possessing the power, or by using more force. It is ironic that peace is also established with truism. This is why, if a man is going to succeed today, he must man-up and take action. He must know how to do it and he needs to witness how other men have done it if he is going to be victorious.

This is where we come in, and here is how to do it with these three easy steps. Taking action is the first and most important step.

Whenever you're confronted by a conflict, take action and take charge a man must act if he is going to survive. Don't spend a lot of time trying to understand the other person's reasoning or point of view. Let them talk with their therapists if they want to be understood. Take action on your own terms. You decide what to do, how to man-up and how to handle the situation. Let your conscience be your guide, and do the right honorable and just thing. Remember: there is no honor in attacking the weak and violence is not what manning-up is all about, and it is not the answer for solving all of your problems.

"Well done is better than well said."
Benjamin Franklin

Recently there has been a lot of to-do with the bullying of others in the news. This really speaks to me, because I have always tried to champion these kinds of people. It is tragic that they feel that they have nowhere to turn and that they are helpless to the cowardliness of being bullied, with the only alternative being to kill themselves. The media's answer seems like a sure-fire way of causing only more pain and problems for these unfortunate persons. This must be a very terrifying feeling to be helpless and feel alone. The media has been broadcasting numerous so-called experts and doctors and such that have been saying "Don't engage the bully," "report the bully" and several other peaceful options that basically say don't "Man-Up" and don't confront. Does this message work?

Is this the historical method of resolution? No, it's not; it's horseshit and it makes the victim even weaker and is a sure-fire prescription to ensure that the person being bullied will continue to be a victim and a target with a big bulls-eye painted on their back for even more harassment. Run, don't stand up for yourself and be a tattle-tale and let someone else take care of it…that's the answer?

I have a different solution and this is where we come in. It is a man's duty to protect the weak and to help them by setting an example of what it means to take action. It is not nearly as important what the outcome is, but rather, whether action has been taken. The coward or bully understands this and will respect this action and respond usually by retreating.

Unfortunately, for the desired effect, an ass-whipping is usually required. It's the only thing that they understand. But, wouldn't it be wonderful if everyone could just get along and we could negotiate everything?

Tell that to the family of Daniel Pearl: the innocent photojournalist who had his head chopped off with a sword and videotaped by Muslim terrorists, wearing masks, whose sole intentions are to kill every American, including women and our precious children. Apparently their God has instructed them to do it.

Now, I don't know about you, but I cherish my children more than life itself, and I love my wife with the same burning intensity of the sun. And I take those kinds of threats personally and would willingly and eagerly march into Hell itself, bare-handed if necessary, and destroy anyone or anything that ever threatened their safety. Do you think that negotiations and talking nice to these kinds of terrorists, as President Obama and Nancy Pelosi have suggested, will actually prevent these insidious and heinous pariahs of humanity from committing more of these egregious, horrible acts while they laugh at us and our rules of political correctness?

Is talking the answer? Will talking nice and trying to reason with another human being that could commit such an act of hatred work? Or perhaps a different message should be sent to show what we are thinking, so they can better understand our position, and to give them a picture-perfect example of what manning-up really means. Personified, and demonstrated with extreme prejudice, and without hiding behind a mask so they look directly into the eyes of our American military heroes who are completely capable of demonstrating what we do to murderous thugs who prey on the innocent and weak, that cannot defend themselves.

Until we reach world peace and universal love through some kind of simultaneous mind magic, we had better concentrate on our continued existence as Americans if we are going to survive and defeat these fanatical murderous bastards!

In closing, I am reminded of a story I have told my five sons many times as they have grown. It is the story of "The Hero and the Coward." I cannot remember where I first heard it, however it has made an indelible impression that I have never forgotten, and I believe it to be astonishingly correct. The hero and the coward are different, yet exactly the same. They both are afraid, except for one monumental difference that will decide their fates and possibly there very existence. The Hero takes action! Period. He does something...there's nothing more to it than that, and that, my friends, is the only defining difference. It's exactly what manning-up is all about.

Let's review:

Step one: "How To Man-Up." This is the short, condensed, easy to understand version! Don't be afraid to take charge, and take action, to show the world you're not pussy-footing around! Stop trying to understand and reason with an idiot, and don't worry about their feelings. Get to the point, and do the right thing and mean it. I guarantee you, whoever you are "manning-up" to might not agree with you, but they will respect you and will definitely know that you still have a pair and are indeed a man. Or perhaps, a very strong, capable woman who doesn't even need balls!

"The only thing necessary for the triumph of evil is for good men to do nothing "

Edmund Burke

CHAPTER 3:

RESPONSIBILITY AND ACCEPTANCE

Probably the single most-often heard, and most important reason for someone not to man-up is having to face the responsibility. And accepting the consequences of our actions that are going to have to be endured in the aftermath of the event, whenever a man chooses to stand up and declare his position. It's not the circumstances; it's the aftereffects that trouble the minds of men. Fear is the deadliest black widow of all poisonous mind-spiders, and is our greatest enemy. Courage is the fire that can forge a man's skin into hardened steel that cannot be bitten, and it's the same courage that is the only deciding factor of whether or not a man can actually defeat all of his fears.

Many times it is this that decides whether or not they live or die. There is a tremendous difference between the man who is afraid and the man who isn't. It's crystal clear, and easy to spot, the confident characteristics of such a person. It is the willingness to accept whatever happens regardless of the outcome. To be able to look down on the spider, and know that she cannot harm you because you are a man and take full responsibility for whatever happens. Now that's courage, and throughout our history as men, we have always needed this attribute to survive, and we need it now more than ever. A man must be able to fully control his minds thoughts and be able to command this quality at will.

Men are being attacked from all sides, and need the courage to man-up and take action, and to be willing to accept the responsibility for their actions. The founding fathers of this great nation demonstrated such a courage and manned-up in a way the world has seldom ever seen or equaled.

The rewards and fruit of their accomplishments are why this country has become the greatest nation and civilation in the history of our planet. The reward was our freedom, that was bought and paid for with the blood and the lives of countless patriots, who sacrificed their hearts and souls for a better life for all Americans. These awe-inspiring men were giants in the courage department, I assure you. Look at what they did and try to imagine how they stared down their fears. Talk about facing down responsibility: they literally took the bull by the horns and then grabbed the bear by the balls, all at the same time!

All of the signers of the Declaration of Independence were successful, wealthy, aristocratic, educated men, who basically signed their own death warrants and were all willing to give up all of their money, property, and worldly possessions...while at the same time committing treason, against England as they pledged their lives in writing! It is almost unfathomable the strength and resolve these men showed as they directly and defiantly said F.U.; and bring it on, as they flipped the bird to the greatest military force in the world and didn't blink an eye.

"What you do speaks so loudly, that I cannot hear what you say." *Ralph Waldo Emerson*

Incredible and true. Now that is really how to man-up, American style. You have to be able to say I just don't give a damn. This is what will happen if you decide to attack me, and you'd better be prepared, because I am not going to idly stand by while you threaten me, my family or my country with harm. There is a price to pay, and I'm willing to pay it!

"The price of greatness is responsibility."
Winston Churchill

I was raised in Cass County, Missouri (correctly pronounced Muzzorah), the sacred home and birth place to some of the toughest, most naturally fearless and aggressive men and women I have ever known. We are just suited for that sort of identity and we wear very well and with great affection. It is a fact that we started fighting years before the civil war actually started and continued for years after as well. That was especially true in the area around where I was raised, near the Missouri-Kansas state line. Cass county was a literal hot-bed of activity and is of historical significance. Missouri was a border state during the war and the fighting in some cases pitted brother against brother.

There were many famous and infamous events that transpired before, during, and after the war, and the men who participated became as famous as the events themselves. The famous James and Younger gang, for instance; Jesse James and Cole Younger are from the exact general area where I was raised. The Younger's are actually from Cass County and Jesse James was from two counties to the north in

Clay County. I am often reminded of those days, and have wondered what it must have been like to have lived through the countless battles and events behind enemy lines and the countless enemy incursions.

Quote: "Since 1865 it has been pretty much one eternal ambush for these two men--one unbroken and eternal hunt *twelve years long*. They have been followed, trailed, surrounded, shot at, wounded, ambushed, surprised, watched, betrayed, proscribed, outlawed, driven from State to State, made the objective points of infallible detectives, and they have triumphed. By some intelligent people they are regarded as myths; by others as in league with the devil."

"Noted Guerrillas" by John N. Edwards,
referring to Frank and Jesse James

These outlaws are considered heroes where I come from, and Jesse James was not the deviant, cowardly psychopathic murderer portrayed by Brad Pitt in the recent Jesse James. movie.

Here are the actual events and real history of how and why it happened, and I am pleased to share with you the story as it actually happened...and its relation and importance to this chapter. After the war ended, the James' and Younger's, along with many others, were declared criminals and considered outlaws for their participation in the war as guerrilla soldiers. Many of their enemies still wanted revenge and so did these men. There was still a lot of bad blood between the Union and the Confederate sides after the war.

The movies **The Outlaw Josey Wales** and **The Long Riders** are both excellent portrayals of the mood and feel of the time. The same soldiers that fought for the Union and committed the same type of aggressions against the South were all given amnesty and/or pardoned. Even after Union soldiers burned down a jail in Kansas City that housed the innocent women and relatives of confederate soldiers, they were let off the hook. Meanwhile, our boys were to be imprisoned and hanged.

The raid on Lawrence, Kansas by William Quantrill, is considered to be the icing on the cake, so to speak, as to why the James' and Younger's were not forgiven. Because Frank James, Cole Younger and a 16 year old named Jesse James were all there at the time of the raid. And, for the record, they absolutely did not kill every man, woman, and child in cold blood on the streets of Lawrence, Kansas, that fateful day. They did however target all men and boys who were of age to have been able to fight and were ordered to show no mercy. Cole Younger was witnessed to have personally saved several peoples lives during the raid.

Quote: "A trifle atrocity prone..."

"That could be said of Quantrill and his raiders, but it could also be said of his opponents. The Lawrence raid came after numerous female relatives of his men were arrested (just for being relatives) and killed or maimed in the collapse of the building in which they were confined. The collapse may have been accidental or not. The raid on Lawrence, Kansas

45

didn't come out of the blue or without motivation. It was one in a long string of atrocities by both sides that had been taking place in the border area since 1854. The prison collapse wasn't the sole reason, only the finally trigger. The response to the Lawrence raid was Order 11 which forcibly depopulated several Missouri counties of anyone sympathetic to, or suspected of being sympathetic to, the Rebels, turning the area into what was called the "Burnt District.".

William Pennington

NOTE: Order number 11, was where martial law was executed and enforced upon the citizens of Missouri. And it was focused primarily on the citizens of Cass, Bates, Jackson And Vernon county's which was where the James' and Younger's and other known guerrilla soldiers and their families resided that gave them refuge. Their families homes were to be burned and their property and livestock confiscated if they were Southern sympathizers or thought to be. Its implication was a horrific display of government control and its plan to de-populate the area by any means necessary.

There were numerous other deciding factors as to why they started robbing trains and banks; and Jesse James actually did try to surrender, but was shot in the chest and almost died as he rode in to surrender under a white flag. But the real reason has to be the refusal to give up and not give in to the Union's demands for surrender. They were defiantly willing to accept the consequences and continued to fight, using the best and perhaps the only methods that they knew, which were to rob and plunder using the guerilla fighting tactics. They learned these and used them during the war against the very same former enemy that had tried to destroy their former way of life. They already knew how to fight, attack and escape the enemy at will with lightning speed, and they were damn good at it. Why not, and who could stop them? Especially considering that they were still all wanted men.

These men had become something totally different than what they had been as a result of their experiences during the war. They were not murderous bandit criminals that went about the countryside, mindlessly terrorizing and robbing the citizens of Missouri, before the Civil War. They were law-abiding, upstanding citizens that came from respectable families. The Younger's father was a public leader, successful businessman and mayor of Harrisonville, Missouri before he was murdered by Union soldiers who wanted revenge against his sons. The James' and the Younger's were fighting against the Northern bankers, railroad barons, and Pinkertons who still represented the North…the same enemy that symbolized the hatred and carnage that was inflicted upon themselves and their loved ones.

In their relentless pursuit of the gang, the Pinkerton detectives threw a bomb into the James family farm home, while Jesse and Frank were away. It blew their mother's arm completely off and killed their mentally handicapped, little brother while they were both in bed asleep.

Now, what would you have done? And what do you think was on their minds? Well, if you have never met anyone from my neck of the woods, I can tell you exactly how those men felt and what they were thinking. The James and Younger boys would never have tolerated such a despicable and heinous crime, and the chances of them turning the other cheek or pursuing some other peaceful solution never entered their minds.

These were fearless warriors, hardened men of action, who were incredibly brave and that had encountered and survived countless life-or-death gun battles. And their enemies coldly stage a sneak attack and tries to kill their mother! Jesus Christ, it was their mother!

There was only one way of dealing with men who could do such a thing. The only thing that those Pinkerton men, with such a lowly pedigree, could ever understand. It certainly wasn't motivation for the gang to surrender and give up or negotiate and talk nice. They were pissed off way beyond any imaginable description, and, poised with an indescribable motivation and furiously angry for revenge, they fought back.

Plainly speaking, they all would have had to have been killed in order to have stopped them. This is yet another reason why they traveled as far North as Northfield, Minnesota and ultimately, that is where the James and Younger gang was basically destroyed. It marked the end of their free reign of mayhem against the Northern sympathizers. Cole Younger was shot eleven times during the Northfield, Minnesota robbery, and lived.

Severely wounded, shackled, and bloodied from all of the bullets in his body, he defiantly summoned the courage and strength to stand and tipped his hat to the ladies as he was taken into custody, as they paraded him and his brothers, Jim and Bob Younger, through the town. He served twenty-five years in prison, and then returned home to Missouri, where he once again reunited with Frank James, who had surrendered his guns to the Governor many years earlier. In the movie, **"The Long Riders"** Frank announced to the Governor, "I'm here to surrender my guns and I want to bury my brother." The Governor replied, "What if I refuse?" Frank replied, "Then, I will kill you."

Quote: "I have been hunted for twenty-one years. I have literally lived in the saddle. I have never known a day of perfect peace.

Frank James

Frank James was also tried in a court of law, twice, and was never convicted for his crimes. That historical fact alone tells you what the people of Missouri thought about Frank James. They couldn't find a jury to convict him.

Jesse James was murdered, shot in the back of the head in St. Joseph, Missouri by the hired assassin Bob Ford. He was paid for by the governor of Missouri. Bob and Charlie Ford thought that their deeds would bring them fame and fortune. Instead, they brought them neither. They were constantly ridiculed and harassed as cowards for shooting an unarmed man in the back.

Charlie Ford couldn't handle the guilt and committed suicide not long after Jesse's murder. A few years later, Bob Ford was murdered, and to this day he is still despised for his cowardly deed. I can still hear the song that was playing on the jukebox at the Oasis tavern south of my hometown, Belton Missouri when I was a child, "The Ballad of Jesse James", and the lyrics about that dirty coward that shot him down.

I still am awe-struck and amazed at the resolve and dedication these men displayed in their willingness to go down fighting, with no regard to their own lives. Their dedication was perhaps misguided, but their determination is inspiring to me because of the passion and immense bravery that it required. Can you imagine the nerve and composure it took to attempt something so brazen? As compared to the hardened criminals of today, who shoot and miss and often end up killing or injuring innocent bystanders. Then, they often elect to kill themselves rather than face the police honorably and go to jail.

This story's relevance and importance are in the message of accepting responsibility, and it's not about the Civil War, slavery, right or wrong or even whether they were justified in their actions. And I am not advocating unnecessary violence, or saying that stealing is ok if the circumstances are right. These were men of action, who lived and died with that same furious passion. They were committed and steadfast in their dedication to each other and their families, and they were willing to accept their fate and took complete responsibility for their actions.

They are prime examples of exactly how and what it means to man-up, and they did it all on their own terms. I respect that. Personally, I have a deep, sincere admiration and understanding for these men, and their exploits are remarkable and legendary mainly because they are not fictional characters from some book. They were real men, from my home and birth place. I admire these men not for what they did or the crimes that they committed, but for who they were. And it is my prayer and heartfelt wish that my nephew, Jesse James Cunningham, and my youngest son, Cash Michael Cole Parrish, who have both been named after these men, will aspire to grow up to be of the same caliber of man. That they will know exactly what it takes and what it means to take action, take responsibility and not ever be afraid to man-up!

Having said that, let's review! Again, here is the short version: Face it! A man has to be willing to accept responsibility for his actions and be willing to handle the consequences. Don't be a wimp! Fear is a black widow spider, and she's a crazed bitch from Hell, so look that bitch right in the eye and then squash her! That's how you accept responsibility…conquer fear and man-up!

"It is by going down into the abyss that we recover the treasures of life. Where you stumble, there lies your treasure."

Joseph Campbell

"Whenever a warrior decides to do something, he must go all the way, and he must take responsibility for what he does. No matter what he does, he must first know why he is doing it, and then he must proceed with his actions without having doubts or remorse about them."

Carlos Castaneda

CHAPTER 4:

KILL KILL KILL!

This is the third step to successfully achieving your man-up diploma. If you have already read the previous chapters, and are confident in your belief that you have mastered them, you already have learned the necessary skills and you know what it takes. So now, I would like to share with you, and this is very important, another part of my man-up psychology.

"Kill! Kill! Kill!" are the exact words that I want to use to describe the next step. They describe the intensity that is required in your mastery of the third step. The third step is about conviction and passion.

It's kind of like the Duke, John Wayne, in his Oscar-winning performance in the movie **True Grit**, when he single-handedly faces the bad guys in that beautiful valley. He is outnumbered 4 to 1, and is accused of making "Bold talk for a one-eyed fat man!" With the moment of truth at hand, he replies, "Fill your hands, you son of a bitch!"

He says this with instant heroic man-up-ness! Not even the slightest hesitation. He boldly takes the reins in his teeth and charges his trusty steed, Beau, fiercely into a dead run firing his revolver in one hand, swinging and cocking his rifle with his other hand, rapidly aiming, shooting and galloping all at the same time, with incredible precision and speed defeating all three men, and at last rises victoriously.

True Grit…now that movie title really says it all. That scene was inspiring, a really good example of good triumphing over evil, and the exact measurement of appropriate retribution, in dealing with such adversaries, given the situation and time period. This scene is very powerful and really epitomizes what I am trying to say. It wasn't about what happened…it's how it happened and what they did.

On both sides. The bad guys manned up too. They just got themselves shot and killed, but they took action, accepted responsibility, and rode, fought and died with passion and commitment, and did it all on their own terms. Perhaps they read my book? Bad men usually do man-up. It seems to be a lot easier for them because the second step is usually already evident to them. They already accept responsibility for their actions, because they are the ones starting the shit! Unfortunately, it's the righteous, conscious man with the strong moral beliefs and self-control that has trouble sometimes allowing himself to overcome his caution and reserve.

Or, how about the young man, Tommy, who was considered a weakling and a yellow coward by town folk his whole life, as described in the song "The Coward of the County" by Kenny Rogers. He sings, "But look, Old Yeller's running, but you could have heard a pin drop when Tommy stopped and locked the door!"

Yeah, anyone could see that those Gatlin boys had that ass-whipping coming. Those guys deserved it for what they did to Becky, and Tommy wasn't fooling around.

Raping your woman is pretty much grounds for that kind of hostile reaction. Tommy didn't waste a lot of time talking either. (Please refer to my 1st chapter, section A, on not wasting time talking to an idiot.)

Both of these examples are great, but my favorite is from the George Lucas classic **Star Wars** movie, when Yoda is training young Luke Skywalker and says, "Try not…either do or do not. That is all." And Skywalker replies, "I don't think that I can," and Yoda replies, "That is why you fail." This is how it must be done. Either do it, or do not. It is that simple. It is also a fact that Lucas was influenced tremendously, when he wrote **Star Wars**, by the great writer, Joseph Campbell.

A man must commit all of himself with complete confidence or he is certain to fail. Yoda knew how to man-up and was trying to teach Skywalker that manning-up was really a life lesson and was just another way to be able to tap into the Force. Those Jedi warriors really meant it. They did all of it with a decided purpose. And they made their decision based on what they wanted and not what another person demanded from them. This is excellent, and so well thought out as crafted by Lucas; and the unequalled success of the film, and the basic root of the story, are both obviously proof that people respond to this theory. Can the gazillion people who have seen this wildly popular movie series possibly be wrong? No, they couldn't.

"It's not what you know, it's what you do with what you know."

unknown

This is absolutely essential in the manning-up mantra. What I really mean to do is to demonstrate another important part of the system. And that is, that a man must truly believe in himself and possess the conviction and dedication, execute the effort and determination, on his own terms. It is that very essence of thought that is necessary to complete the process of mastering your emotions. First, by taking action; second, by accepting responsibility and overcoming the fear of reprisal; and now, third, by doing it and meaning it with power and determination. Being able to accomplish your goal, using your own self, to guide your conscience and, hopefully, to be able to instantly ignite the supernatural forces that all men have within their minds.

I'm talking now about all of the millions of years of genetic memory that all men share. This is a concept that I have given a lot of thought, because of its significance and its overall importance to all men, but I will briefly touch on the subject later, in more detail, in chapter 9 "The Natural Order."

Basically, it is the innate sensations and familiar feelings…such as the moment-of-truth feeling, the kill-or-be-killed feeling, or the fight-or-flight feeling. Some men are more focused and in tune with this philosophy and others are simply more in tune with the universe, but one thing is for certain: we all are able to feel it, because it is there. It really is kind of a force that I believe to exist in us all, and we all can draw upon its power. And if you don't feel it or can't seem to tap into it, then perhaps you should put the bong down and stop smoking weed, or drinking yourself into oblivion, if that is what is keeping you from moving forward. Concentrate, and you too will be reunited with the mysterious and magical mancestry of awesome horsepower that is necessary to put yourself into high-gear, and dig yourself out of the rut you are in. Drugs and alcohol are not the answer to enlightenment. Your mind is. You are in charge! You are responsible for your own happiness and success. Stop blaming others if this is what has been impeding your growth, mastering yourself and dedicating your energy and man-power for the greater good, which is harmony in your life.

Believe me, I have extensive previous experience in regard to this subject, and I know how you are feeling; if this is indeed your problem, and the reason you cannot man-up and move forward is because of the self medication you have been prescribing for yourself. It's a endless circle, and I have personally been to the fiery pit and can feel your dread. But it doesn't have to be that way. If I can do it, and Keith Richards can get sober after everything he has injected, smoked or swallowed into his body, then you certainly can muster the strength to man-up and take the stage. Christ, Richards was pronounced dead four times! The poor guy has a face that looks like a hundred miles of bad road, but he has continued to carry on and has manned-up for decades, and he is still rocking. He has to be pushing seventy. Age is only a number.

 "It's only rock and roll, but I l like it, like it, yes I do!"   *Jagger and Richards*

One of my childhood heroes and life mentors once said: "If a man has done it , then it is possible, and it is done; if it is impossible, then it shall be done. "

I'm sure that he was quoting someone else, because Evel would have had to have been just about completely hammered on shots of that 100 proof Wild Turkey that he used to drink to have come up with some super philosophical shit like that. Basically, what he was saying was that as men, we are unstoppable. When he said it and he had to have believed it wholeheartedly he literally was unstoppable. At that time, he was the coolest hero America has ever known. He was an original American icon and was more famous than Elvis at the time. And, just like me, every kid in America was building homemade ramps, jumping and flying through the air on their bicycles in the street, trying to emulate our hero.   I still have some pretty amazing photos of my greatest childhood jumps.

He was very patriotic as well. He spoke of education and family values, and proclaimed his stance against drugs. Perhaps this was a bit hypocritical, because he partied like a "Kennedy" on spring break and is legendary for his appetite for booze, wild party nights and for his conquests of hundreds of beautiful women even as he was totally against illegal drugs and their hippie culture. Later, in the winter of his life, he would require a liver transplant because of all of the blood transfusions, and he contracted Hepatitis C, but drinking all of the alcohol certainly couldn't have helped, and he said himself that the Wild Turkey was partially to blame.

He was also disgusted by the outlaw motorcycle culture. While performing a jump at the "Cow Palace", a member of the "Hells Angels" motorcycle gang threw a tire iron at him, Knievel went into the stands and punched the guy out. Evel later said in an interview that he always wanted to punch one of those guys in the face and was more than willing to go even further. He also said that he actually felt sorry for the poor bastard, because the fans in the stands continued to go after him and just beat the hell out of the guy. Maybe he should not have thrown that tire iron? Some people just do stupid things.

Anyway, Evel is single-handedly the father of today's extreme sports, an innovator, and he was a leader and pioneer light years ahead of his time. Think about it: here is a man who created an entire genre. Most of the jumps he did had never been attempted before, no one had ever seen such a thing, and they were all incredibly dangerous. Certain death was very much a possibility.

If you don't believe me, go to "YouTube" and watch the film of his jump in Las Vegas, in 1967, at Caesar's Palace, and the horrible crash that happened. He was damn near killed and spent a month in a coma. The fact that he survived, continued to jump, and continued to survive spectacular crashes, countless injuries, multiple compound fractures and broken bones, is nothing short of remarkable. And he did it on a 500 pound Harley Davidson motorcycle.

It's nothing short of amazing and there hasn't been anything like him since. I have written a country song about him called "The Ballad of Evel Knievel" as a tribute and you can check it out on YouTube.

"A man only fails when he doesn't get back up."
Evel Knievel

There have been four people that have attempted to jump the same fountains at Caesar's Palace. Evel Knievel was the first, and he suffered a crushing wreck. His son Robbie cleared the fountains perfectly. He also later accomplished pretty much everything his father was unable to do. Another daredevil didn't make it and was horribly injured. Finally, Mike Metzger, superstar motocross and stunt rider, performed an amazing backflip in astonishingly perfect style.

However, the stars of today have today's equipment, and that makes things totally and completely different. The ramp's speed and trajectory is calculated with computers. The motorcycles are incredibly light and super fast Evel Knievel had none of those things, not even a speedometer. He did it all by feel and his bikes were like slow-flying refrigerators with wheels by comparison. His contributions and achievements are the story of a real legend. Once he committed, there was no backing out. And he never did. If he said he was going to do something, he did it. Some would say that making such jumps is not really a sport. Well, maybe it's not a sport, because you can practice a sport.

Most of the jumps that he performed could not be practiced or rehearsed because of the obvious danger involved. Many times, he was so badly injured that death was a real imminent reality that had to be wrestled to the ground or absolute failure was the only other option. Evel always backed up what he said. He was a man who put his money where his mouth was. He walked the walk, talked the talk and always backed it up. He was a man of deliberate action.

I remember the time he was arrested for beating up a writer who had made some terrible and untruthful remarks about Evel's mother and their relationship. Evel was mad as hell, and told several people he was going to beat the hell out of the guy that wrote those lies about his mother…and he did. Evidently, "Shelly Saltman" wrote a book and had tried to capitalize on and exploit Knievel's success, and he had probably said those things in order to sensationalize and sell his bag of lies and it made Evel furious…

Well, Knievel was textbook old school, and didn't take kindly to this guy telling the whole world that he hated his mother. So, in vintage and classic Evel Knievel fashion, Evel took a bodyguard with him to the 20th Century Fox studios lot in Hollywood, California, and found Saltman. Knievel then took a baseball bat and mercyisly beat him unconscious. Knievel smashed and broke the guy's arm so badly it would require surgery. This attack just wasn't a public bitch slapping, it was an all out ass-whipping.

Evel said he took the bodyguard because, at the time of the attack, Evel had two broken arms that were both in casts and he was afraid that Saltman might be able to take the baseball bat away and use it on him. Evel was arrested and went to jail for the offense, but NEVER once apologized for the attack, even at trial. How's that for personal conviction and passion?

He was later sued and found liable for millions of dollars in damages however, the writer never received a penny, ever. It was pretty much the end for Knievel as far as sponsors and endorsements went, and his meteoric rise to success, but he was quoted in later years as saying he wouldn't have changed a dammed thing, and he was glad he did it.

I also have a friend Brook Hansen, and his father Paul Schmier, was there and eye witnessed the event. His story is one of my favorites, and I cherish the privilege whenever he shares and relives the story with me.

I personally had the privilege of meeting Evel in Kansas City, Missouri, in the early nineties. He was driving a black four door Masarati with his soon-to-be wife, Krystal. They were in town hustling golf and gambling. I owned a bar, in south Kansas City, **"Michael's"** and he was there with a very well-known underworld figure that is actually in Nevada's Black Book, and I will not disclose his name here, but perhaps another time.

However, I was completely star-struck. Mr. Knievel was incredibly gracious and polite. And he was very funny.

My partner, AKA "The fastest fist's on Broadway" and also another very important life mentor to me Tommy Ribaudo, who himself is famous in Kansas City and is considered to be a legendary club owner, ladies man, fist-fighter and a real life kind of "Italian Stallion" so to speak, were both manning-up to each other as two super-alpha male game cocks often do, whenever they have met their match. And they were trying to best each other as they were comparing their war stories, when Tommy said to Evel, "I almost broke my back jumping over the bar to get at this guy" and Evel instantly replied, almost? "I have broke my back five times!"

This was an incredible night and Evel was amazingly entertaining with the stories he told. He totally exemplified the legendary man that I had always thought he was. It was also very apparent that Tommy Ribaudo and Evel Knievel were actually very much alike and became instant friends. To this very day it still makes me smile.

I got to meet and drink scotch whisky with one of my childhood heroes and it was an experience that I will never forget. The world lost a real man's man when Robert Craig Knievel passed away, We shall miss you. Rest in peace, Evel. I wonder if the writers of today and the over- zealous paparazzi would behave the way that they do if there were more Knievels around, knowing what consequences lay in store for their actions.

And perhaps…when the very sad day comes that Tommy Ribaudo is gone, I will be able to finally divulge the almost unbelievable and incredibly fascinating true stories about Tommy, and I can share Tommy's real life adventures and our friendship of how this man trusted me, took me under his wing, believed in me and mentored me into becoming the man that I am. Believe me when I say that have I got some great stories to tell...

Look, it doesn't take a rocket scientist to figure this out or how to do it. But you do have to really believe in yourself. Seeing examples, and copying other inspiring men and their accomplishments, will show you and help guide you, but in the end, it's all up to you to take the handlebars in your hands, pop the clutch, hit that ramp as fast as you can, and hang on for dear life. And if you happen to come up just a little short, and sail over the handlebars head first, to resemble some kind of helicopter kamikaze-style rag doll, with your arms and legs flying in all directions, and you end up busted, broken, bloodied, and crushed on the concrete, don't worry...because you have already "manned-up" and you have done so with passion. Now get back up and do it again!

Let's review. "Kill! Kill! Kill!" doesn't mean for you to go postal or completely berserk. It means that this is the level of intensity that is needed to kick maximum ass. It is the third step to successfully manning-up. It is having "Conviction and Passion" in what you're doing and how you do it.

Commit and either do or do not, young Skywalker. And may the Force be with you.

The Man-Up Force, that is!

"Passion and conviction are powerful weapons against an enemy who depends only on fists or guns. Animals know when you are afraid; a coward knows when you are not."

David Seabury

"It is the repetition of affirmations that leads to belief. And once that belief becomes a deep conviction, things begin to happen."

Muhammad Ali

CHAPTER 5.

MAN-UP ON YOUR OWN TERMS

The fourth step is the easiest one to accomplish. The previous steps are perhaps a bit more difficult, but are the basic roadmap to successfully being able to transform even the most sheepish man into a Tyrannosaurus Rex of testosterone, of manliness and power. Whenever you do engage your new powers, you must do so on you own terms. Affirm that you are the captain of your universe, and refuse to be controlled by anyone or anything, and you will have completed and mastered the message of this book, young grasshopper.

Look at what's going on around you, and you can decide for yourself. It's all around you, everywhere. All you have to do is open your eyes and look. Men are being persecuted, and we are not being allowed to be men. Outside forces are trying to change us into something we are not, and portraying us as weak and feminine. That's what this book is about. It's about being able to stand up proudly and act like a man should, to be able to distinguish the steps that have to be taken, and doing those things on your own terms, not mindlessly obeying the other side or the dictates of the conflicting opposition, whatever that may be.

A lot of men, especially young men, are being targeted for this, bombarded with pictures, sounds, and images of false and submissive males on TV, in movies and commercials, and in magazines.

The media is very cleverly trying to disguise its flagrant brainwashing, by actually identifying part of its plan. They do this by giving it a new name, designed to confuse people and to win the approval of both men and women, and to gain acceptance of it by calling it things like the new "Metrosexual." They tell you about the wonderful position you will have in society if you conform to this new, androgynous type of identity and lifestyle. Metrosexual…what the hell does that even mean?

I believe that it is just another attempt to try to destroy the male role model and that what it really means is that men need to stop exposing their natural qualities, and stop identifying with other traditionally strong alpha male types. And that it is ok for men to act and dress more like a woman. That society will reward you for it, by giving you everything that you have ever wanted. And that you will be very cool, and liked by other men and women, and that if you exhibit and show qualities of both sexes, it is perfectly normal and widely accepted.

But if you don't agree, or don't accept this label, and you show any signs of manliness by not agreeing with or obeying their commands, they will attack you. And if they decide that you aren't sincere enough in your apologies or your commitment to the cause, they will accuse you of being, or label you as, being a bigot and racist or some other kind of politically correct assshole name that they have invented, that most men cannot even understand.

Then they will compare you to others on TV, to make you look like some kind of weird super-charged Nazi male supremacist that hates everyone else on Earth, and who is secretly mean to puppies when no one is looking! And then, finally, they are going to plaster your face everywhere, for the entire world to see, so that they can all gang up on you at once. Kind of like a gang of rabid zombie cheerleaders, who are all journalism majors and are currently experiencing a very intense menstrual cycle.

What they are really saying is that we men have basically been doing everything all wrong. Who is responsible for this bullshit? Who are the persons behind this campaign? Who, and more importantly, why are they doing it and why are they trying to change men? I already know, and I am doing something about it. And I am doing it with zeal. I fully know what it is and who is responsible. My mission is to try to help inform you, and to give you a clear playing field so that you will see this for yourself, and to be able to decide to man-up, if and when you are called upon to, and to be able to show other men exactly how to do it and what it looks like.

Am I wrong? Is it just me? Well, let's take a look at just one recent event. How about the case of Tiger Woods and his recent marriage problems? Here is an example of what happens when the media gets its taste for blood in the water and when they know full well that you are already wounded, and that you cannot stand up and fight back.

They are the worst kind of enemies, because they get the luxury of playing both sides. But be very careful, because the big smiles, full of shiny white teeth, are actually hiding their fangs, and behind that pretty white smile, they can turn and bite you just as fast as a rattlesnake if given the opportunity. Why? To get better ratings than the other guy, regardless of whose life they destroy.

They prey upon the weak and the helpless, while they glamorize other persons of very superficial character and they encourage our children who are watching to copy, admire, and emulate someone who has never accomplished or actually contributed anything of tangible merit to the world, but who still has become a famous celebrity simply because their daddy is rich. Or, more commonly, because their sex tape that was stolen. You no longer have to be talented or good-looking, or have any admirable qualities, to become famous, and look who is making all of this possible. The media glamorizes these people and then they watch and wait for their victims to be weak and fall, because it is sensationalism and it encourages more people to watch. They do all of this while hiding behind the guise of "it's a story and the public needs to know."

They argue that it somehow justifies the carnage of their deeds, and the pain that has been inflicted upon someone else's life, even though their reputation is utterly destroyed forever, and they're forgiven because of it. Why did they destroy Tiger, after they raised him to such biblical status?

Because he let them do it to him. Because they knew that he had too much to lose; in Tiger's case, possibly hundreds of millions of dollars. His camp, and his genius handlers, called it damage control. I am truly sorry that his father had already passed…perhaps he could have inspired his son to have manned-up, and things would have been vastly different. Unfortunately for Tiger, he has become a perfect example of exactly what not to do and how not to do it.

Here is one of the richest and greatest athletes in the world, and a role model to millions of kids around the world, and he is caught and put on 24-hour, round- the-clock carnival display, prodded and poked non-stop in front of the entire world. Then, it is proclaimed by the media experts that, "Not only are you a multiple award-winning adulterer and a complete failure as a husband and father, but now, we'll label you with another one of those super-cool, politically correct, mumbo-jumbo names that we have concocted and call you an uncontrollable sex addict!"

Yes, ladies and gentlemen, the media's experts and doctors have all decided that men who can't control themselves, and who want to have a lot of sex and really like it, actually has some kind of horrible, contagious disease. That's right, it's a disease! Apparently, the person that has their finger on the "let's make up a new addiction and give it a name" button has decided that if a man actually likes women, wants more than one woman, and just can't ever seem to get enough poon-tang, it is because it is an actual disease, that requires treatment with doctors, medicine, and apparently a hell of a lot of therapy! Shocking but true. I told my father this story and he promptly replied, in typical Les Parrish fashion, "Yes, son, I know all about it. Who do you think was the one who gave it to him?" I guess old Tiger's rampant marital infidelity had absolutely nothing to do with his wedding vows or his commitment to his loving wife, or a general lack of self-control and will power, or the dozen other reasons that have been accepted for the last two thousand years.

The absurdity of this explanation is above and beyond all reason. If it were true, then every man with a pulse has it, or at least, that is what my wife says. And I must confess that I must be terminally ill, as I have been hopelessly infected with this terrible affliction since the age of 5. And it seems to get worse by the minute. After being married for 22 years, I still simply can't resist, and have a constant, burning desire to tackle my wife whenever possible.

However, I don't dare actually perform such an action with anyone else other than my wife, for fear of hearing these words coming from her mouth as I lie in a pool of my own blood, while she assertively asks: "How do you re-load this damn thing?" So I don't.

This is another pristine example that the media has invented, of how they're saying that if a man cheats, maybe he couldn't help it. He is just very sick. This is so stupid it boggles the mind, and is also why I have very little belief in, or respect for, any of the so called experts, doctors and talk show hosts.

Why would a famous fashion model be qualified at giving parental advice to impressionable young girls...when she has no children? Now there is even a former security guard from the "Jerry Springer show" that has his own show. These so called experts spew out their advice with machine-gun, rapid-fire answers as fast as the geysers at Yellowstone. Who in the hell told these people that they should be giving advice? The "wisdom" of these knowledgeable experts is often mind-boggling.

As Tiger submitted to this abuse, he professed at his televised crucifixion/apology that among other things he will continue to seek the medical treatment that he needs (thanks a lot, Dad!), and that with the help of his mother and God, he hopes to one day return to golf. When I saw that apology on TV, I wanted to break the friggin' TV set. Not because of Tiger and his personal problems, I couldn't care less about that, and it wasn't any of my business anyway who Tiger was screwing. I've never met the man.

No, it was the furious rage I felt for him, because obviously he simply did not possess the will...or even worse, the knowledge to have manned up and to have told the media that it was none of their business. That this was between him and his wife, and to kiss his ass! If he had done that, he would have shattered and shocked those bastards into retreating as fast as they could run...hopefully back under the rocks where they live.

He would have shown the world that he was indeed a real "Tiger", and not the terrified little kitten that he appeared to be. He lost all respect and credibility at that very instant for millions of people.

Except for Nike; they seem to think that having a person with such admirable qualities is excellent, and that he will continue to sell even more shoes. Those same Nike executives, however, had the audacity and unbelievable gall to actually use a commercial with Tiger's deceased father's image creepily hovering in the background, as if it were some kind of weird beyond-the-grave consolation of Tiger, with his father's approval of the events that had taken place. It sickened me, and his wife as well, because it was reported that she refused to have any part of it, and she promptly divorced Tiger following these tragic events.

A word of warning! Whoever is giving Tiger advice is someone you should stay away from at all costs, if you are in any way remotely affiliated with such people. I am sure that they all have several college degrees, and I guarantee you that the ringleaders and smartest ones are all doctors. And as we know by now, the willing participation of doctors in the brainwashing of men makes everything else they say highly suspect, to say the least.

I do have one word of encouragement and advice for you, if you are ever put into a similar situation as Tiger's, do not follow any of Tiger's methods for solving your problem, because, as a man who had the chance to demonstrate to the entire world his resolve and strength as a man who could have really manned-up and defended himself and his family...he has completely failed in every sense of the word.

However, his beautiful wife, the woman who was betrayed and humiliated through the lens of the world's media showed an overwhelming toughness and power that is to be admired and emulated by men and women everywhere. Her actions are identical to the lessons and instructions that are prescribed in this book, and she definitely knows how to man-up. And, she did it on her own terms.

I do feel pity for Tiger and for his wife. It is unfortunate that they were not able to save their marriage. Just think, all of those millions and millions of dollars and still it couldn't buy themselves happiness, just as the old saying goes.

All married couples know that a real marriage is a fully equal partnership and that it requires hard work and trust on both parts to be successful. However I can see why it happened and hopefully now you can too and that you can decide for yourself if their story is relevant to this chapter.

"Inaction breeds doubt and fear. Action breeds confidence and courage. If you want to conquer fear, do not sit home and think about it. Go out and get busy."

Dale Carnegie

"Boldness be my friend!"

William Shakespeare

CHAPTER 6:

WISDOM AND COMMON SENSE

I am sure that I will be attacked from many sides because of the aggressiveness and tone of this book. If I am attacked, or discounted as being something other than what I am, it will be because they really are not seeing the message or getting what this is all about. I am not advocating unnecessary violence, and I am not preaching hate. And I also don't care what they think or say about me because as my mother always told me…"The birds only pick at the best fruit."

What I am doing is saying it is time to man-up; that it's time for a revolution, to revolt against what's going on, with the clear message and advice on how to fix the problem, by using the most efficient and direct method I am aware of. The steps that have been outlined in this book will show you how and why, but it is your conscience that should govern all of your actions.

> "The cyclone derives its power from
> calm center; so does a person"
> *Norman Vincent Peale*

A smart man must also learn to use his self-control whenever he is switched into "man-up"mode. I have had to learn the hard way on this in the past, many times, and can tell you from experience about what can happen if you let yourself run completely amok, without controlling your emotions.

On the one hand, we, as men, are designed to be able to carry the sword, start the fire, build the roads, to be aggressive; to be able to fight and to sustain ourselves, and to protect our families. On the other hand, we are also gifted with the ability to practice control over those very same abilities, by using our self-control. It's the kill switch that shuts down the engines and cools the motor from burning itself up. A blown engine is unable to start, or to be able to finish the race, and is therefore of little value to the owner. Men seem to be able to understand this simple concept, but it is an effective metaphor for this chapter's message.

The Bible is the most respected, and most clear, example that I can possibly use to illustrate this, and there are countless answers in the Scripture that would serve us all to memorize and to be able to use at our discretion. However, my favorite one is: "Do unto others as you would have done unto you." The purity of that one defining statement is so powerful and clear. That one statement would completely resolve and put an end to all of the world's problems if it were only enacted. Imagine yourself being treated with such respect, and the harmony that would be created by everyone following such a simple rule. The entire world would be different.

As men, however, it seems much more difficult. Why? Because we project unto others our own opinions and what we think they should be doing, and how they should act. The desire to control the thoughts and minds of our fellow men, and the intrusion of their beliefs on others, have been the major causes for the problem since the beginning of time and are also the biggest reasons why I have been compelled to write this book. A man has to be able to stand up and rise to the level that it takes to sustain himself, and to continue on as a man, but he must also use his common sense to guide him through the events he encounters in his life.

Manning-up isn't about fighting, unnecessary violence or acting like some kind of jerk that has just learned how to mentally overcome his fear, and show everyone that he is a bad ass. It actually means the complete opposite. A real man only uses his power, confidence, and strength to save himself or others. **He/She is a champion against injustice.**

My favorite poem reflects this, and its relevance to this is remarkable and so beautifully written that I have enclosed it in its entirety as follows.

Hell! There *ain't* no rules around here! We're trying to accomplish somep'n.

Thomas Alva Edison

IF
By Rudyard Kipling

If you can keep your head, when all about you
are losing theirs and blaming it on you;

If you can trust yourself when all men doubt you,
but make allowance for their doubting too;

If you can wait and not be tired by waiting,
or being lied about, don't deal in lies;
or being hated, don't give way to hating,
and yet don't look too good, nor talk too wise;

If you can dream–and not make dreams your master;
If you can think–and not make thoughts your aim;

If you can meet with triumph and disaster
and treat those two impostors just the same;

If you can bear to hear the truth you've spoken
twisted by knaves to make a trap for fools,
or watch the things you gave your life to broken,
and stoop and build 'em up with worn-out tools;

If you can make one heap of all your winnings
and risk it all on one turn of pitch-and-toss,
and lose, and start again at your beginnings
and never breath a word about your loss;

If you can force your heart and nerve and sinew
to serve your turn long after they are gone,
and so hold on when there is nothing in you
except the will which says to them: "Hold on!";

If you can talk with crowds and keep your virtue,
or walk with kings–nor lose the common touch;
If neither foes nor loving friends can hurt you;

If all men count with you, but none too much;
If you can fill the unforgiving minute
with sixty seconds' worth of distance run;

Yours is the Earth and everything that's in it,
and–which is more–you'll be a Man, my son!

I am also reminded of a personal story, something that happened to me over thirty years ago as a young man. The lesson that can be shared with you now is about how common sense in manning-up played an important role in the events of my life that were to later unfold.

I was working in a bar in Kansas City, Missouri, while I was still in high school. I was eighteen years old at the time. I really wasn't even old enough to be working in such a place, since it required everyone to be twenty-one years of age to get in. I had been the apparent object and target of a much older man's hostility, the source of his anger. I didn't really know why he disliked me so much, but he really seemed to hate me for no apparent reason. I have my suspicions, but I hadn't specifically done anything to cause his bullying and hatred. The guy just didn't like me at all.

However, at the time, I have to admit that I was tagging anything that moved as far as the ladies were concerned, and he wasn't much of a ladies' man to compete with, so to speak, so perhaps that was the source of his anger. Finally, he followed and cornered me one night and we got into a slight physical confrontation. Now, at eighteen, I was six feet tall, but only weighed one hundred and forty-five pounds...and although I wasn't afraid to fight anyone, I was severely outweighed and outgunned by this much older, bigger, more experienced and more mature grown man who had insisted on fighting me.

This bar was really a lot like the one in the movie **Roadhouse**, and I was nothing like Patrick Swayze or his character when it came to fighting. I was in the big leagues, right smack in the middle of the adult jungle, working and making moves in a bar that wasn't a place for the weak.

This was 1980 Kansas City, Missouri, and these kinds of men don't mess around when it comes to showing some young punk who's the boss! The pushing match was stopped almost immediately by the bar manager and a couple of the bouncers, but this guy who started the damn thing was a regular customer and a good friend of everyone there, so he wasn't asked to leave.

He just smirked at me and smiled, and said to me and everyone else in the bar how lucky I was to have survived, because of his Vietnam hand-to-hand combat training and experience, and the death and carnage he had inflicted upon others, who had not been so lucky as to have been saved before they had the shit kicked out of them.

Well, that was the final straw as far as I was concerned, and the beginning of his demise. You see, my father was, and still is considered a kind of legend where I come from. A notoriously violent fist-fighter and "cocksman", who had many well known admirable qualities, yet he especially had completely mastered two well-known abilities and attributes: fighting and drinking, and he was excellent at both. Besides being a very large man he was very athletic and had the fastest hands I have ever seen. He was a marvelous specimen of a man.

Whenever it came down to kicking the shit out of someone, the old man was famous for his incredible lightning speed and ferocious anger. He scared other, very-well-known, tough guys into running a lot of times...I know this to be true, because my mother was there and witnessed it. He and my mother divorced when I was a baby, but I always knew about the stories that were being told about my dad. People actually stopped me on the street and asked if I was his son.

Describing my father at the time is very simple. Sandy blonde haired and bright blue eyes, six foot tall and about 225 pounds, very broad at the shoulders and narrow at the hip. And he looked like he was chiseled out of a piece of granite. Most people, especially women, considered him very handsome, charming and funny. And his hands were absolutely huge, his fist's looked like 8 pound iron-sledge hammer's. He is of Scot-Irish and Cherokee descent and was one of eleven children, and he left home at twelve years old. At sixteen years of age, he was a buck sergeant in the United States Marine Corps. Papers were forged and he served admirably during the Korean war.

All of this foreshadowing is necessary, because what happens next is very funny. I immediately called my mother after these things had happened, and told her that "I've had it" with this jackass and to call my dad. I had seen his truck earlier that evening at a local roadside bar, and already knew he was probably drinking and where he was. At the time I thought that this was a good idea...I was wrong.

She first   hesitated and said a strong word of
caution, because, as she said, "You know what will
happen." "Yes, I do", I replied. "Call him." So she
did. Thirty minutes later, I looked out from the stage
where I was performing, and there he was…and I
will never forget it. It was my dad, and he was
standing in the middle of the bar and thunderously
asking, "All right, where is this son-of-a-bitch? As
he scans the room from side to side and then says,
"And tha…tha…tha…that…I am going to tear out
all those God-damned disco lights!" (My dad
stutters' when he drink's!)

I almost died right there. If I were to compare it to
anything, it would be like seeing King Kong tearing
his steel his chains loose and getting ready to
destroy New York. I, and everyone else who heard,
was instantly terrified of what was going to happen.
I jumped down from the stage and met him halfway
across the middle of the dance floor, and promptly
lied, telling him, "He's gone, dad, the guy has
already left." Knowing full well as I did so that this
guy was sitting at the end of the bar and didn't see
what had happened through the crowed room.

Next, my mother arrived, and the manager and
several cocktail waitresses, who knew my father and
what kind of bodily injuries and property damage he
was capable of, tried to calm this terror, and
mountain of man, into simmering down. He was in
rare form and I was there to watch it all unfold. He
was ready for anything and after all my wishing the
moment of truth had arrived and now I wanted no
part of it. Honest, I was really afraid that he would
kill someone and it would be my fault.

Now, at that moment, and as I returned to the stage and prepared to get back to work, I watched my dad and mom as he did finally calm down, and everything seemed like it was all going to turn out fine. No one was going to be beaten to a bloody pulp. No one was going to need the assistance of an ambulance or paramedics, no one would possibly be in a coma or have to move with the assistance of a walker for the rest of their lives, or at least, for the next several days, as possible consequences from what could have happened. I had just successfully lied to my dad, and truthfully, had possibly saved another human being's life. But then, all of a sudden, I look out across the dance floor to the bar and I see Mr. Jackass laughing, mocking me as he flips me the bird.

KABOOM! Something snapped, and I could not stand even one more second. I pointed to him to meet me at the front door and marched straight to it. I was met there by one of Kansas City's police officers, and another bouncer, both of whom knew what was going on by the time Mr. Jackass finally got there. I rapidly started telling this idiot that I had saved his very life and that I had even lied to protect him from a beating that would have surly ended his Vietnam-storytelling days forever…when he cockily says to me and the policeman, who knew full well who my dad was, "Just who the hell is your dad?" The cop instantly said, "He is definitely someone you don't want to mess with, and someone I would never mess with unless I had a death wish."

And at that very instant, I saw an expression of wide eyed fear in both their eyes as they turned and saw my dad standing in the doorway. At that moment, all courage and all prior display of this guy's posturing was completely gone. Sucked completely out of his body, like by some kind of vacuum. My dad looked at all of them, instantly pointed to each of them, and asked, "Wha, Wha, Which one is it?" The bouncer, the policeman, or Mr. Jackass...it didn't matter. Whoever it was, was about to be killed.

They were all scared shitless! They each looked like human bobble-heads as their eyes were bobbing back and forth, wide open, and they were looking at each other like they all wanted to point their fingers at each other, and I held that power in my hand as I reached over and pointed my finger straight at the guy, and said, "Him!" With that identification, and instant lighting speed, my dad's hand shot out like a jack-hammer, grabbed this poor guy's neck, and started to crush his throat in it...his hand lifting him completely off the ground, with one arm, and the other cannon cocked back and ready to fire!

But wait, not so fast! Now it was time for the public humiliation to commence. My dad then commanded me to "Come here, Mike, come here," while the other two men stood in shock and did nothing, absolutely nothing, to stop him. And, much like a grizzly bear teaches its young cubs how to catch and eat fish that are helplessly jumping up the river, my dad wanted me to hit this helpless fish as Papa Bear made sure he couldn't move.

Right at that moment, I knew what I had to do. The lesson was a life-changing event, and I had to man-up if I was ever going to be a real man. So I refused. I said, "No, dad, I'm not doing it." I simply could not bring myself to hit a defenseless man, no matter how he had acted. He was already beaten beyond anything I could have ever done to him, anyway. My dad kept trying to get me to do it, but I kept refusing his commands. My father finally let him go and told him that if he ever saw the guy again, or if he ever bothered me again, he would stick the guy's entire head through the keyhole in the door. That was the end of it, and he never bothered me again. But, the story isn't finished there, though.

Fifteen years later, fifty pounds heavier and having had survived many bar fights and other harrowing experiences, I was a vetted, much older and much wiser man, and now actually owned a different bar and nightclub only a few miles from where this had all taken place years before.

It was at the end of the night, and I was working the door when I thought I recognized someone drinking at the bar. So I approached the disheveled, old and tired-appearing man, who seemed to look very familiar to me. I casually leaned over and I instantly recognized his face. It was Mr. Jackass, and he wasn't the same man who had earlier been so eager and willing to kick my ass, to say nothing of having been quite capable of it. But now things were far different then they had been years earlier and this was to be a completely different story.

He appeared small and weak. I smiled and knew what his fate would have been if I so desired, but no…I didn't believe in that kind of revenge. Instead, I calmly asked him if he knew where he was and who owned this joint, and said confidently do you remember me? He said, "No, I don't!", as he smirked and scowled with his same usual attitude. "Who's asking, and what's it to you?" And once again I thought, I cannot take this, especially after what he had already done and how I'd once had him right where I could have destroyed him, and now I held that same power in my hands. So I looked at him and said, "My name is Michael Parrish." And he instantly replied, "No…but I sure as hell, remember your Dad!" And that is self-control and common sense, as best I can ever describe it to you. That's how to man-up and do the right thing.

There are so many other stories about my dad that could fill entire volumes of books, and I will definitely write his life story because it is so much better than anything Hollywood could possibly dream up. And the amazing thing is that they are all true. Countless, tales of women, money and adventure!

My father has lived an amazingly storied life that in many of the cases, it doesn't even seem real. People often just stand there with their mouths open in shock and bewilderment and hang on every word as I entertain them with his exploits. He is a very unique person. He has perhaps, made choices that have come back to haunt him, (although he would never admit them) but I have NEVER seen him bend to anyone ever and he has a strength and power that is usually only known to exist in books. He is now in the winter of his life and it will be a very tragic day for my wife, our children and myself when he is gone. Once as a young man we were arguing about nothing and I sarcastically replied to him in a heated exchange "how do you know so much and what makes you think your right?" He calmly raised his brow stared me directly in the eyes and instantly replied, "because I am older than you, I know more than you and I have lived a hell of a lot more life than you!"

I was awed at this reply, because I had been soundly beaten and his words and its beauty and purity was so eloquently spoken. I simply smiled at him and said…you are right. And he was. I worship my father and I don't think he realizes how immensely important he has been to me and my family. My wife also loves him deeply and considers him her father as well.

"Setting an example is not the main means of influencing another, it is the only means."

Albert Einstein

"Better than a thousand days of diligent study is one day with a great teacher."

Japanese
Proverb

CHAPTER 7:

BE AN EXAMPLE TO OTHERS

According to the Chinese calendar, 2010 was the "Year of the Tiger." This year should be a very good year for those individuals who have been fortunate enough to have been born under its protection and symbolic meaning. The cycle is repeated only once every twelve years. Interestingly, the Chinese calendar can be traced as far back as 14 B.C., but legend has it goes back much further to the year 2637 B.C. Throughout history, tigers have held important associations in Chinese culture. For instance, the meaning of the tiger in Chinese culture is usually power, force and strength, and the tiger is usually depicted in art and idioms as a metaphor for those ideas. I encourage you to **Google** the term to learn more about it and to read about the character traits of the tiger. It is a very interesting read.

In Imperial China, tigers were the representation of warfare. While the emperor and empress were embodied as the dragon and phoenix, the highest army general was usually depicted as a tiger because the tiger's fierceness and courage were similar traits to an army commander. The tiger is also considered the "King" of all animals, and tigers are still known today as the ancestral gods of Chinese culture. (General information taken from the Internet)

I am fascinated by the Chinese and their accomplishments, and the vast, perhaps endless, contributions that they have discovered.

They are a remarkable and ancient people who have a rich and interesting past. Their quest for knowledge, and their work ethic, are widely known and history has been recorded it as such. A very large part of their culture is to emulate others and to lead by example.

So my fascination with yet another one of their traditions, and its comparison to this particular chapter, will be my focus and message in your "How to Man-Up" bible.

I am reminded of the story of Sylvester Stallone and how he made it after years of knocking on doors and trying to make it in Hollywood, and his incredible persistence and determination that was to inevitably prove, way beyond a shadow of a doubt, that he was indeed committed. I will use Stallone's own account and personal recollection of the events that had happened from an article that I had read which covered the story. I believe it was Cigar magazine.

The story goes something like this: Sly was living in L.A. and had been auditioning for years and trying to make it as a movie star. He had some minor success, and had gotten a few good roles, but stardom was still very much way out of sight. As he tells it, he was an unemployed actor, almost completely broke, married with a baby, and had few options at his disposal. Now here is where the true content of this man's character really starts to shine. You see, Sly had an excellent imagination, and in his mind, he knew what he wanted to do. And what he did was text book.

He decided to copy and emulate what other successful writers had done to reach their goal, and that was, to write a vehicle to propel himself to stardom, because no one else was capable of executing such a task. This is how "**Rocky**" was born. Sylvester Stallone wrote the inspiring story as a means to make himself a star and the rest of the story is even more fantastic.

Can you just imagine how he was able to just arbitrarily one day decide, "Hey, I think I'll write a movie to make myself a star, and win the Academy Award at the same time." Here is a guy that says to himself, "I'm completely broke, about to be evicted, with a wife and a baby and no job, sounds good, why not?" So he did!

This is how things unfolded and the story gets even better from here. You see, Sly was at an audition (though he didn't get the part) and had just finished writing the script, and as he was walking out the door, he paused, turned and said, "Oh, yeah, I'm also a writer." The producers were suddenly interested and said, "Really? What have you written lately?"

He had them at "hello." You see, almost all producers and directors are also writers, and that has been their method for success. Hollywood has always been in search of talented writers and they were instantly interested, because they totally understood as one writer to another, and they wanted to know more. The rest of the story is off the chart as far as balls are concerned, because it basically went like this. They immediately offered him $15,000 dollars for the script and started shopping it to all of Hollywood's "A" list leading men, who at the time were Burt Reynolds and Ryan O'Neil, among others. These producers knew that they had a magnificent story on their hands, but they also had absolutely no intention of ever letting its writer, an unknown actor, star in his own movie. But wait, not so fast; these men had obviously never been in the presence of someone who could have easily have offered lessons on "How to Man-Up" and what it looks like in Technicolor.

They were about to be taken to school. The offers continued to grow and the amount was continuously refused. Over and over again, Stallone kept saying no, no, no, until it finally reached the all time highest price ever offered for a movie script in Hollywood, which at the time which was reportedly $300,000 dollars, Stallone simply said a repetitive "No, I want to play Rocky and that's it, take it or leave it."

This is Biblical, because of the overwhelming temptation that he was facing, but he held his mud, and the rest is movie history. He has gone on to write and star in many more movies, and his book is great for any man who wishes to know his private secrets and proven methods for keeping in shape and staying on top of your game for men after age 40.

Bottom line: Sylvester Stallone followed the example of others who had played this very difficult and tricky game, and ended up creating an entire dynasty. And he has become an American hero to fans all over the world.

Ironically, Sly's character, "**Rocky**," is seen proudly wearing a beautiful satin jacket in the second movie, which displays a beautifully embroidered "Tiger" on the back. Well done.

There are other famous men whom I admire and who have also shown to others that you can be an example and still keep and hold your ground.

Mel Gibson is such a man. Although recently he seems to have completely lost his mind a few times as reported in the news. (Please refer to chapter 2 in regard to what we men are capable of doing, because of a woman!) Am I telling the truth or what?

However, you can't help but like the guy, even if he has used poor judgment. He is a man; we make mistakes and he has certainly had his share lately, but to my knowledge he has never run from any of his responsibilities, and he continues to man-up on a regular basis as far as I am concerned.

Good thing that I wasn't the one they caught drunk on that video, because I would have actually made Mel look good! I have demonstrated more than once what a total jackass I can be, and the problems and havoc that I was responsible for because of my actions of mayhem under the influence. We are all human. It is our character that defines us, and what we repeatedly do is who we really are. Not one moment in time, it is the life and the total journey that makes men who they are. Not a 30 second "YouTube" clip.

One remarkable event that happened in Mel's life was his decided commitment to make the movie **"Passion of the Christ."** It was the story of the crucifixion of Jesus Christ and it was an extraordinarily visual and graphic description of this Biblical event. It was a portrayal of Jesus' suffering, and the unequalled and excruciating cruelty, hatred and horrible pain that was deliberately inflicted upon him and what he was forced to endure.

This movie created a very disturbing unease and induced screams for mercy from most everyone who saw it. Even the coldest, most unfeeling and callous human being could not possibly handle watching it without feeling a great sadness or compassion for him, as he was relentlessly humiliated, tortured, and then was finally nailed to the cross. It was an extremely emotionally charged film. I cannot think of any other movie ever made that could equal its power and ability to evoke such sympathy and emotion from simply watching it.

He was told by many so-called movie insiders that the movie would be career suicide and his career would be over if he dared to make such a film. He shopped the movie and was turned down by every studio in Hollywood. Even though he was one of the biggest box office drawing stars in the world. They all refused. He was also accused of being a racist by certain Jewish organizations and others because of the film's story and content, before the movie was even made. He was unfazed by all of this and went on to make the movie anyway, using his own money and the rest of the story is in the history books.

Because it grossed almost a billion dollars, proving them all wrong, and was a tremendous success, if you are to use Hollywood's own gold standard for evaluating success. Which is to say, money earned.

The skeptics were all proven wrong. This happens all the time, and is a clear message, that there are a lot of people who have ascended to their position and status in life that have no business being there, as I have stated. It is a fact, and almost anyone who has ever made it can testify to this and could tell you the same type of story that happened to them. It has happened to me, many, times, almost my entire life in different forms. And I, too, many times before have proven them all wrong.

The answer to their apparent tries to impede anyone's effort is one very simple task, and that is, to never stop. That is the only time a person can ever fail to reach their goal. Mel Gibson still continues to make films, and his career was not damaged in the slightest. Personally, I hope that he finds balance and harmony in his life, because he is an excellent film maker that can encourage men to aspire to be more than they are. That's what many movies really are: they are dreams and inspirations materialized and captured on film. I hope that he can continue to be powerful force and a prime leading example to men, because we need him to do so.

 "Ask not what your country can do for you, ask what you can do for your country."
John F. Kennedy

Speaking of actors, a couple of months ago, my wife and I had the pleasure of seeing something very remarkable. We were invited guests of Tony Baca, Operations Director, for Sharon Angles campaign and we were present at a political rally at the Orleans Hotel and Casino here in Las Vegas. There were several speakers that were scheduled to speak at the event, including Sharon Angle, who was running against United States Senate Majority leader, Harry Reid; Michael Reagan, Former President Reagan's son; Arizona Senator John McCain, and legendary movie star Jon Voight.

It was a very inspiring evening and there were several thousand people at the event. The message was very clear that evening. These people from Nevada were very angry, and the source of their anger was Harry Reid. Nevada has been the hardest-hit state in the entire nation as far as the recession is concerned. And Las Vegas is the leading city in all of America for unemployment, foreclosures and several other categories of troubles and hardships concerning its citizens. It has been devastating for many, and personally for me and my family as well. My wife and I have basically lost everything we have worked for the past 20 years.

As each speaker took the stage, the applause was deafening and there were at least a hundred reporters there from all over the country recording every moment. I have a very personal opinion in regard to Senator Reid and if you have already read the **Dedication** at the beginning of the book, you know what I think of him and why, so I won't repeat myself.

But this chapter has a relevant message related to this evening's events as they were to unfold, and will serve as another excellent reminder of how a man must focus himself to be an example to others and the obvious importance of that ability.

Now, I have always liked Jon Voight as an actor, and have seen most, if not all, of his movies. **"Midnight Cowboy"** and "**Deliverance**" are classic movies that are considered required study in most film Schools, and there are other Jon Voight films as well that show his tremendous talent and ability to bring a character to life on the screen. He is an **Academy Award** winner, and is considered by fans around the world to be an iconic figure. I believe this to be true, and I do not use this term lightly, because to me, an icon is someone who has repeatedly displayed their accomplishments for a very substantial amount of time, and they have somehow changed the order of things in a monumental fashion that will stand the true test of time. It has infuriated me in the past as I have heard others use it when describing almost any minor current celebrity, so it has lost its true meaning.

This man is a real movie star, who has been at the absolute top of his game for decades, and is still currently working. That fact in itself is amazing, considering the general life expectancy of today's movie stars. And I am aware of his relationship with his daughter, Angelina Jolie, who has herself become a superstar and is also a very gifted and a remarkably talented actress, besides being one of the most beautiful women on the planet.

As a father of two daughters, believe me when I say, I can relate to the challenges every man is faced with when it comes to handling their children, especially girls. It can't be easy, especially if you are constantly in the public eye. He also has seemed to take the high road whenever he has been prodded by some reporter's jabs in regard to his relationship with his daughter and has never fallen into their trap.

If only others would take notice of his example, perhaps we wouldn't have to hear men completely break down, go astray, and try to deflect their adulterous escapades by blaming their actions on some tragic lurid childhood event that had happened to them and that was the secret cause of their adulterous behavior. Case in point: Jesse James and Sandra Bullock. But that is another chapter entirely.

I had always known that Jon Voight was a strong leading man and driven character actor, but I had no idea who this man really was until eye witnessing it that evening. As he took the podium everyone in the room was silent as he began to speak. And as Jon Voight began to speak, I was completely moved. He was one of the best, if not the very best, orators I have ever seen or heard and he wasn't reading from a teleprompter as President Obama has obviously mastered.

Previously, I had thought that President Obama's acceptance speech, when he received the party's nomination at the Democratic convention, was the finest, as close to perfect, speech that you can ever get. It was almost too perfect. And I have extensive professional public speaking experience, so I felt qualified to make such a judgment.

However, my mother told me that she personally thought that Martin Luther King and John F. Kennedy were both much better speaker's and that was because they were more natural. She was right. She also had observed, and told me, that Obama was obviously reading from an eye-level teleprompter, and that he was being cued to change and look at the precise moment into the other camera. Go to YouTube and watch it for yourself, and you will see the difference. No wonder he was so good.

But this wasn't a politician reading from a teleprompter; this was a citizen. He spoke with the utmost truth and intensity, and whoever had written his speech was also truly magnificent and an excellent speech writer. If Mr. Voight had written his own speech… (as my wife has predicted)… then he could very easily have made a career out of it. It was direct, funny, entertaining and right to the point. His message addressed the climate of the nation and he predicted exactly what was going to happen on Election Day. And it did happen.

Unfortunately, Sharon Angle wasn't elected, but the message that was sent on Election Day to Nancy Pelosi, President Obama and the entire Democratic party was received loud and clear. That an "old fashioned shellacking" (according to President Obama) was what they had received.

We sat there listening to this speech and I couldn't help but think out loud to my wife, "Wow, he is really excellent!" The crowd was on its feet every time he made a point and the applause never stopped. He continuously attacked Obama and said exactly what was on his mind.

He didn't jack-around, either, as so many speakers do, who are afraid of really saying what they think. Jon Voight was on fire and the audience that night would have gladly followed him anywhere he had chosen to take them with his message, and I would have been right there with him. "Fierce" would describe his delivery. "Tiger" also comes to mind.

This symbolic image would later resonate even louder as my wife and I relived the moment only a few days ago. We were still moved by his words and his inspiring devotion to America several weeks after the rally. My wife never ceases to amaze me and had said to me before that there was something very similar between the two of us, me and Voight.

I could have walked on water right then and there! She was comparing this awesome movie star to me. I am still smiling, but I thought that she was kidding or just being complementary. However, after she had said it she also said that she was serious and that there really was something there, but she didn't know exactly what it was.

So, as usual, to prove her point, she turned on her psychic female super-powers and boldly predicted that Mr. Voight and I were definitely of the same sort of clan and that we were somehow truly connected. After a few minutes, she then fired up the laptop and **Googled** Jon Voight's birthday and we instantly smiled in perfect unison and harmony. Then she proudly proclaimed, "Told you so!" Once again, I was shaking my head in total disbelief. She was right again. I thought, "Damn, how does she do that?"

You see, Jon Voight was born in 1938 and according to the Chinese calendar it was "The Year of the Tiger." I was born in 1962, and I too was born in the "Year of the Tiger." I have always worn this symbolic symbol with extreme personal pride and this was our year! Oh yeah, Evel Knievel was also born in 1938. What are the odds?

So my wife's ego boosting was a wonderful compliment and I am deeply humbled by her humorous comparison's. For my birthday this past year she hired a tattoo artist to come to our home and I had a killer "tiger tattoo" inked on my left arm as homage to 2010 and its sentimental meaning, before I had written the book.

I am now even more impressed with Jon Voight, and the fact that he is surrounded by the most enflamed, extreme, left-wing liberals on the entire planet! Hollywood, California is the epicenter and is considered holy ground zero for these hardliners. A place where he has engraved himself as one of their own, yet has also at the same time defined himself as a leading crusader conservative protector and is also one of Americas most famous celebrities. Not only has he merely been present, living and working in that jungle among the jackals of these extreme liberals, but he has thrived and flourished for decades. And he has stalked and taken his prey at will, whenever he chooses and at his own discretion, unfazed and unharmed.

"Be bold and mighty forces will come to your aid."
Basil King

How in the hell can he do that? I know how, and if you had witnessed his passionate speech, you, too, would know. He has no fear; tigers do not conform to such things. They are bold and rebellious and always land on their feet. This is why I have described him and the patriotic encouragement that he has inspired in my wife and myself.

If you were to apply all of the chapters' lessons of this book and compare the two, Jon Voight would be considered a vetted, samurai-master of man-up-ness, instinct, knowledge, and personal power. He is an outstanding example of how to man-up and defines this chapter's title with exquisite perfection.

I also find it very ironic, and I now wonder constantly if his famous daughter even really knows, that her father is a tiger, and that the huge tiger tattoo on her back was somehow placed there by the universe, and that it is really her loving father, protecting his child. I wonder if it is a sub-conscious symbolic message that he will always have her back, no matter what happens, as fathers and tigers always do. Or is that the real reason why she had it done in the first place, already secretly knowing in advance as my super-psychic-powered wife has predicted?

Regardless, it just goes to show you that "God works in mysterious ways."

CHAPTER 8:

MENTOR

I have been lucky to have had several incredible and different mentors during my life, and recently I have been praying desperately for my one true master, teacher, and life mentor to appear to me. I keep seeing in my mind Tom Laughlin, in the title role in the movie **Billy Jack,** and in my mind, I can see him dancing around in that pit as he lets that huge diamondback rattlesnake bite him over, and over, and over, again and then rising and standing majestically, high above on that rock ledge, as the morning sunshine cleanses his spirit.

He symbolically conquers all of his fears and he survives the test after being bitten six times. He is enlightened, and the vision of the "Great Spirit" comes to him and they become one. Man, that's one hell of a hard way to become enlightened!

This was awesome metaphoric symbolism for millions of young boys. I saw this movie when I was 10 years old, and I can still remember it perfectly. I was so inspired by its message and identified with it very much. I respected his courage and strength, and his ability to try and defeat overwhelming odds.

Back then, that kind of thing is what young boys were taught. We were mentored as boys into becoming men and to aspire to be something good. To be proud, bold, and strong.

In the movie, he knows that he cannot defeat an overwhelming number of men who have savagely humiliated and attacked a group of children, but he willingly accepts the challenge as he walks into the middle of all of them alone, and confronts the leader of the racist gang of town folk. The over-confident adversary says to Billy Jack, "Do you really think that all those Green-Beret karate tricks are going to help you against all these men?" Billy Jack comically shakes his head and replies, "Well, I guess that I don't have much choice, do I? So you know what I'm going to do just for the hell of it?" He smiles. "I'm going to take this right foot and whop you right on that side of your face, and you know what?" Billy Jack asks "What?", the smiling gang leader says. Billy Jack replies, "There's not a damn thing that you can do about it." "Really?", replies the gang leader. Billy says, "Really."...... WHOOOP!

I became a full blooded Indian at that very moment. Movies can make a very strong impression, especially on a child. Which is why this is so important. Where are the mentors, and what has happened to men showing the world who we are? Are Orlando Bloom and Johnny Depp even remotely believable as swash-buckling, strong, alpha-male type men who are actually capable of such feats, as they prance around and sashay in such an obvious manner? In the past movies didn't portray men like they do now. Probably because they knew that the public would never buy it. Why is it happening now?

In real life this does not happen. Yes, I know that it's a movie, but you get the point. Why are we being portrayed as being passive and why are men so often portrayed as androgynous figures? Strength is not a crime. It is the powerful silent weapon that all men must have in their possession at all times, and know wholeheartedly that it is there. Not having it is the real crime. Using it takes common sense and responsibility, that men should always deploy it only as needed and with definite purpose.

The past few years have been very challenging to me, and at times I have felt lost and not on my correct path. It has actually been longer than that because I have changed career paths several times in the past few years, and now I am doing that very thing once again. I have been very fortunate and blessed to have had the innate ability to do pretty much anything I set my mind to doing, and it has always been that way. Sports, school, music, work, making money, and women all came with little, but focused, effort and ease.

I just knew that I could do it and believed it. It was especially evident when I was a child and as a young man. Many times I would declare it to be so in advance and would predict the outcome. And in that lies the beauty and magic. It continued into my 30s and 40s…except that now, for the first time ever in my adult life, I have become a little bit more cautious and reserved. Having a very large family, and being responsible for so many people, has finally resonated a sense of "wait and see what happens," and that temperament is not what I have always done in the past. My wife especially has noticed this caution and has said that she has noticed the change. She doesn't like it either. She has said that I need to be myself, but I am still thinking that maybe I should wait and not be so quick to act on my instant impulses and be so quick to react to life's events.

Perhaps so, I am reminded of several of my friends when I was growing up and how they were taught to behave by their parents. I did not have a father at home to teach me and I often identified with the men that I saw around me and what I learned in school. And they were much different than they are today. Men today seem to be much more neutral and almost seem to kind of walk on egg shells most of the time, and are afraid to display their true nature for fear of some form of reprisal. Not all men, but some.

I am reminded of the story about Wayne Newton and Johnny Carson, because you can't always judge a book by its cover. I deeply admire and respect Wayne Newton, because I know and have extensive first hand knowledge of the enormous difficulty it takes to make it in the entertainment business; and Mr. Newton is a giant (who started his Vegas career as a Vegas lounge singer, and so did I) and has defied the odds and has been a starring headliner around the world for the past 50 years...and he is still going strong. The story goes like this: Johnny Carson began cracking on Wayne during his monologues on **The Tonight Show,** and he persisted for several shows. Almost like he was on a mission to try to belittle Newton.

He also started making homosexual innuendos and aiming then right at Newton. I guess the final straw came when Carson was on the air and said something like….

"Wayne Newton and Liberace were found in a bathtub in Vegas,…and…it was pink!"

Newton told the story in his bio and said that he was shocked and couldn't understand why Carson, who he had considered a friend, would do such a thing. Wayne had been on the **Tonight Show** many times and he was not laughing. He might have been seen as a Las Vegas type entertainer who often wore flashy cloths and jewelry, however; Newton certainly wasn't gay and he definitely wasn't a wimp. He had gotten his Black Belt in karate and had said that he was prepared to defend himself to the death if it was ever necessary. Namely, against his own older brother…isn't family great? Also he isn't a small man. I have seen him up close and he is well over six feet tall, and probably weighs two hundred and twenty five pounds, and he wasn't fat.

The next part of the story is symbolic to this chapter, and is an excellent, true example of what a man does when he chooses to make a stand on his own terms.
Its relevance is that his actions are a textbook formula for the mentoring of other men. Wayne Newton could have called Johnny Carson, or perhaps sent him a letter, or even had one of his assistants send a message; however, that is not what he did.

He went to NBC Studios in Burbank, California, personally to tell Carson what was on his mind. He walked directly into Carson's office and boldly proclaimed "I don't know why you are doing this, but it is going to stop right now. And if you ever say anything about me again, I am going to whip your ass!" Johnny must have gotten the message because he never said another harsh word about Mr. Newton's sexuality ever again.

Mentoring has always been the method for men to aspire to greatness, and the lack of it today is why we need more men to step up to the plate and to show other men how it is done, and to personally guide and teach them as well. Men need to see strong, truthful leaders who have demonstrated their abilities to the world and adopt students to mentor them.

Men like Nelson Mandela, who is an incredible leader for all men to emulate. He was unjustly imprisoned as a political prisoner for 27 years and prevailed against mountainous odds. He eventually took his true place in society. His courage and strength are immeasurable, and he is a living patriarch of what a hero really is.

And of course the righteous Dr. Martin Luther King, he defines the embodiment of mentoring with a clarity and authority to which there is no equal. He was a very remarkable leader who's holy belief in mans ability to overcome any obstacle is so spiritually inspiring I could easily have written an entire man-up book on him alone.

I mentioned earlier that I have had several mentors in my life, and I have. There have been real, and also imaginary, mentors whom I have often called upon whenever I needed support.

Frank Brunson was a boyfriend of my mother's who took me under his wing when I was a little boy and taught me how to ride motorcycles, and he actually bought me a motorcycle one Christmas and he always treated me like I was his own son. He also served as a role model and I love him dearly.

My father is also a mentor and I have learned many things from his simple but very direct advice. He has shaped me as a man and I owe my strength, courage and hard resolve to him. He gave me a folding four inch buck-knife at 4 years old, my first B.B. gun when I was 5 and his prized Marine Corp bayonet when I was 8 years old. And a .410 shotgun and a .22 rifle and lots of ammunition when I was twelve years old. Yes, I was heavily armed at twelve years old! He has shown me a crystal clear picture of a man that has never shown fear…ever.

Other men in my immediate family, such as all of my grandfathers, my uncles Bob, Johnny, and Homer Parrish and especially my uncle Tom Parrish, have all mentored me. These men are real Missouri men who all define the term "man-up."

Tom Parrish has taught me many things. He is an amazingly strong, confident man, and we are closer than brothers. My uncle Ronnie Parrish taught me how to sing and how to play the guitar when I was 10 years old. He himself is the greatest country singer I have ever heard, and I often compare him to the greatest country singer of all time…

The one and only, George Jones. I am not kidding either, he has a haunting tone in his voice that is one in a million, very unique and different. I and my family truly believe that if he had gone to Nashville when he was young, he would have become a very big star, because back then, especially, male country music singers could really sing and they were all different sounding artists.

In business and friendship mentoring, Richard Reynoso, has been and still is a great mentor to me. He is my "Mexican" dad as I fondly call him and he solidifies this books message. He is also a Republican conservative who became furiously angry at Senator Harry Reid's election comments that all Hispanics would be crazy to vote any other way than Democratic. Meaning that Mexican Americans were to stupid to make up their own minds and that they needed the Government to help them. He was pissed! And I don't blame him, he believes in the American dream and he comes from a very long line of Mexican-Americans who are very well educated, work hard and do not need charity from anyone.

Charles Benjamin, "Uncle Charles" as I have always called him, has always counseled me and has taught me to control my explosive temper and how to keep a cool head in times of trouble.

And especially Tommy Ribaudo, whom I mentioned earlier, was the most important person to have ever wholeheartedly believed in me at a young age, and in my talent and natural ability.

I also learned a great deal about how to treat people, because Tommy is a master story teller and he has a natural charisma and charm that people adore whenever he is in the room. He changes things just by walking in the door. My father has this same ability and they are very much alike in many ways.

I am aware, and realize, that many of my examples and stories are about fictional characters, mainly from movies. This is true and is also why we need to get back to the real type of classic male portrayal and real male characteristics that were once shown in movies. I love movies and I am a big fan of the cinema. I am also an actor and I have been a member of the **Screen Actors Guild** for the past decade.(Well, I was; I'm not so sure if they will still want me after this book is published. Ha!)

But the truth is, I have been influenced greatly by the media's messages that I have absorbed and processed in my mind. There are also many great and wonderful lessons that I have learned from these movies, and from the stories and the actors who played the roles. It has only recently happened, within the past twenty years or so, that movies really seemed to have changed. There are many classic actors and filmmakers that immediately come to mind, men like Steve McQueen, Kirk Douglas, Charles Bronson, Lee Marvin, John Wayne and my personal favorite Clint Eastwood are all timeless. All of these actors represent a certain degree of machismo and have all of the basic "man-up" ingredients and define what this book is really about.

Clint Eastwood recently said in an interview with "Esquire" that he thinks that men have become soft and are now often weak. He is right and he should know, not because he is just some tough guy actor, but because he is 82 years old and has been around a long time and has seen a hell of a lot of life. He is a multiple **Academy Award** winner and is, without a doubt, a proven, vetted screen legend who has made some of the most thought-provoking and interesting films in cinema history. He is a writer, director, actor and artist who doesn't blindly follow others down the trusted familiar path of the trail…he blazes his own.

The final scene in the movie "**Unforgiven**" resonates with a realism that I can only describe as breathtaking, and is the most memorable scene I have ever witnessed. The character "William Munny" slowly rides into town on a pale horse (visually symbolic of the scripture in Revelations from the Bible that describes death and the hell that followed with him). It is in the dark blackness of night as a hard driving rain is pouring down upon him. An empty whisky bottle is thrown to the ground. A sudden bolt of lightning flashes and an eerily loud sound of thunder ominously booms as he walks into a hive of law-men and townsfolk. He is quickly noticed and recognized as the towns-peoples' mouths gape wide open in shock and disbelief, as if the Devil himself had just came to dinner.

Before he speaks, he slowly raises his double barreled shotgun and says, "Which one of you fellow's owns this here shit hole?"

At that very moment, all of the confessions and denials that he had previously proclaimed for the entire movie were instantly over. It had all built up to this one moment. All of his ineptness and general lack of ability were nowhere in sight. His prior denial of how he was no longer the infamous Missouri outlaw and cold blooded killer, whose loving wife had cured him of it, was back! And with him, came an evil vengeance and presence that is rarely witnessed by any living person.

It can only be described as ruthless retribution. His seemingly unbelievable, but sincere intentions, that he had long since given up all of his former wicked ways….were in fact not over and something very bad was about to happen.

Perhaps they might have been over, until his friend was savagely beaten to death and was used as decoration for the town's saloon as a direct result of something Munny had done. Now the moment of truth had arrived…and it was going to be epic. At that moment, Clint Eastwood was William Munny, and it was brilliantly superb.

My reason for going into this is because I had been present and have witnessed actual events and have seen real men in very similar extremely dangerous situations. Not in the exact same detail, but real life or death situations. In some instances, guns were involved and someone could have easily lost their life.

As it turned out, they didn't, but it was real just the same, and I was there and have personally witnessed it several times. I felt the same realism watching Clint Eastwood (especially his eyes) and comparing these prior events of my previous life.

Please do not take this as boasting or bragging, because; I am not proud of many of the things that I have done in the past and that I have witnessed. But; I have spent countless years working in saloons and nightclubs where I have experienced very dangerous mind numbing and horrendous events that most people have not had to be a part of. And I have had many friends sent to prison…including "Death Row" for contract murder. Nevertheless, this movie was as close to real as I have ever seen.

And the movie "**Gran Torino**" (which should have swept, all of the Oscar's) is such a fantastically important mentoring movie that it should be required by law for all men, young men, and boys to watch. Its not about racism, death or any thing else as far as I'm concerned, it is about the beauty and power of being a mentor and the sincere truth of being mentored. It is how the teacher appears and the student and the teacher are both transformed into something else and what it really takes to do so. It is a riveting portrayal that speaks volumes of wisdom, strength and honesty. Mr. Clint Eastwood channels something so monumentally profound onto film that the movie is really something else entirely.

And it has very little to do with all of the character's obvious emotional and character flaws that all men and boys sometimes have. It is the epic story of a realistic tale of mentoring. Identically similar to all of the "Rocky" movies, that were all boxing films, but in reality they actually have almost nothing to do about boxing, and its message is something totally different and much more important. And so is "Gran Torino" and we need more stories and men who can pull it off in such a masculine manner.

The lesson that can be taken from this is that Eastwood has a gift and can tell a story with such vivid amazing detail that he creates unforgettable emotion. I admire that ability and respect his talent and his refusal to copy others and to play it safe. Those powerful male qualities are "Mentoring 101" examples as far as I am concerned.

Here are some very thought provoking and uncanny, strikingly identical words and thoughts from Mr. Dirty Harry himself. His relevant male observations are textbook "Man-tastic!" (Esquire magazine interview.)

"My father had a couple of kids at the beginning of the Depression. There was not much employment. Not much welfare. People barely got by. People were tougher then."

"We live in more of a pussy generation now, where everybody's become used to saying, "Well, how do we handle it psychologically?"

"In those days, you just punched the bully back and duked it out. Even if the guy was older and could push

you around, at least you were respected for fighting back, and you'd be left alone from then on."

"I don't know if I can tell you exactly when the pussy generation started. Maybe when people started asking about the meaning of life."

We applaud you Clint...I could not have said it any better. Now, "Go ahead and make my day!"

"Make no little plans: they have no magic to stir men's blood...make big plans, aim high in hope and work."

Daniel H. Burnham

CHAPTER 9:

THE NATURAL ORDER

Geronimo was a legendary Apache leader who had successfully led his people and who masterfully avoided being captured by the U.S. government for over twenty years. Much to peoples' amazement, he was not a chief. He was a medicine man, a shaman of wisdom and supreme spiritual strength to his people. And rightly so, for he was able to show his people just how capable he was in times of trouble, rather than speaking to them with words or in writing or some other means of communication. He wasn't an elected official that had ascended to this position through some popularity contest or other means.

He was there because he was supposed to be there. And it was his natural place in life as a man, and a man of action. He was respected and thought of as a great warrior who could not be killed. Also, he was thought to be invincible by his enemies. This turned out to be true as well, because after countless battles and life or death confrontations, during many years of seemingly endless and impossible odds, he died a very old man. He was never killed by any of his former enemies. It wasn't for lack of trying, that's for sure, because many had tried. He had previously lost three entire families and countless allies, who were killed and ruthlessly murdered during his lifetime. Just try to imagine having to endure the loss of so many loved ones.

However, they all were unsuccessful and failed at killing Geronimo. He was never even officially captured by the United States government. A military force that was state-of-the-art for its day, made up of thousands of men, that were equipped and trained to be possibly the greatest fighting force on Earth, had been chasing him and his band of elusive renegades for twenty years. Yet, he was only able to be found through the government's ability to trick and convince other Apache scouts into helping them find him. And when they did fid him, and all 36 others that were with him, it was a band of very few warriors; mostly it was old men, women and children that were starving.

The great general only agreed to stop fighting so that he could save the rest of his people. He agreed to surrender at Skull Canyon in what is now known as Arizona. The U.S. Army then "heroically" arrested the very same Apache scouts that had made it possible to track down the elusive war captain and placed them all under arrest. They were moved, shipped by railroad car to Florida like cattle and then to Oklahoma, where Geronimo died a very old man. His exploits as a leader are legendary, and are textbook examples of required reading at today's West Point military academy.

The amazing genius of his natural, innate, superior abilities of skill and cunning in creating and then dispensing tactics of organized guerilla warfare speak for themselves. The devastating effect these things had on his enemies has led him to be considered one of the all time great military generals of all time by many of today's most respected and trained military historians. And, as a warrior, he was considered a ruthless savage who didn't believe in mercy. He was incapable of such an emotion. His ability to deceive his enemies was nothing short of supernatural.

Just think about it. Here was a man with no formal education or training, who only knew and possessed the abilities that had been handed down to him as a child, the basic skills that were handed down for thousands of years from father to son since the beginning of time, yet he was able to elude capture and continue fighting the entire United States cavalry force in the southwest, which consisted of thousands of men with superior training, for twenty years. He was never captured, only convinced to surrender to save others. He accomplished all of this using the technology of the stone age.

Compare this to the weapons training and all other manner of technology that was available to his rivals, and you can see the immense natural power he possessed. I wonder what he could have done if he and his men had been trained, educated and equipped with equal weapons and the exact same technology of the time, and placed on a level field of engagement. What would the outcome have been? Obviously, history would tell a different story.

This is the Natural Order of things, and I want to share this obvious and crystal-clear message of importance and relevance with you, so that you will know the perfect simplicity of its meaning. I will show you, over the next several pages, just who accomplished this, how and why it has been accomplished, and the reason why we, as men, should seek to find our rightful place, and why manning-up is so important.

Have you ever asked yourself, "how in the world did that happen?" Or "how did he or she get to be there?" And "why?" They obviously don't deserve it and I can't understand how this could happen. Or how about, "Why hasn't this other person been placed in his/her rightful and natural position? And why is he or she constantly seen on TV when they aren't qualified for such attention?"

The answer to that last one is simple. It's because they have been unnaturally placed there. I can easily see the reasons how and why. For instance: look at how the media is now manufacturing celebrities and creating stars. You can also see how this doesn't always work. Why not? Because they are not supposed to be there in the first place. And no matter how hard they try, the public cannot always be fooled into believing their bull.

Here's an example: why is it that so many of the stars of the wildly popular "American Idol" never seem to last or are able to sustain their popularity? It is simply because they haven't proven themselves worthy to be in this position. How did they make it, only to subsequently fall and never be seen again, with such ease? Answer: because they were placed there without having to have earned it, and without the proper merit. This happens all the time, and more and more often, the person or persons involved fall out of sight even faster than the person before them did. Countless overnight stars are born for all the wrong reasons, and the universe simply rejects them as fast as they appear. Meanwhile, the worthy and determined candidates must wage war and never quit, because they are being forged by that same universe that says, boldly, "I will allow all of your dreams to come true, but first you must show me that you deserve it and that you will not give up, and you must also be able to tolerate a very long line of complete and total idiots who have no idea what they are doing, that I have placed and marked for you to encounter on your trail to stardom. If you get past these bumbling fools, who are completely ignorant and have absolutely no knowledge in regard to their field of expertise, then yes, I shall yield to you and surrender."

By "bumbling fools", I mean people like the coach who cut Michael Jordan from the high school basketball team, who could not see his future ability. Or the newspaper editor who fired Walt Disney, and told him that it was because he had no imagination. Or the booking agent at the Opry who told Elvis Presley that he should immediately return to driving a truck because he could not sing.

Or perhaps, one of those supremely brilliant record executives from every major label, who had the chance to sign four young lads from Liverpool, England (the Beatles), but just didn't hear any hits on their demo recordings. One record exec even told their manager that "guitar groups" were on the way out! By the way, these were the exact same songs that later sold millions and millions of copies.

These morons have the astute and mind boggling credit of refusing to sign the Beatles, not once but twice; and literally losing billions and billions of dollars because they were in positions of authority and decision making, and they were simply not qualified to be there, they were way out of their Natural Order and correct placement in life.

Another favorite example of mine is the cancellation of the wildly popular first **"Star Trek"** television series. Who ever was responsible (which, obviously were the leading executive's in charge), were all completely out-of touch and incompetent, because; not only did they revive the series multiple times, they have been making **"Star Trek"** movies for the past 40 year's since the original series was taken off the air. "Captain Kirk"...was definitely a turbocharged super-alpha-male who was constantly seen banging different space chick's across the entire galaxy! I even saw one episode when he had a romp in the sack with a very sexy looking alien space chick and she was green! Damn...

This might be the only time I could honestly say perhaps Captain Kirk should have actually manned-down, because that kind of man-up horsepower is really pushing it! (Probably...was a sex addict!)

One other thing I have noticed and have observed is the startling fact and inherent problems that many of today's lottery winner's seem to have after winning millions and millions of dollars. Many lose it all.

Why does this happen? How can this even be possible and what could possibly be the reason for a person to have such troubles? Well, now you know, and it isn't me making this information up, it is a real and genuine fact of the Natural Order of things.

There are countless other stories that are relevant to this point as well, and I could easily write an entire book on this subject alone; however, I will limit myself to getting the message across with just these few examples. However, country star Toby Keith's story is excellent and Toby is a prime example of this very subject, so let me relate that one as well:

Apparently, Toby had been knocking around, trying to make it in Nashville, for several years and finally got a well-respected and successful record executive (appropriately named Buzz) to begrudgingly agree to listen to Toby's song, one that he had written himself. Toby was laying it all on the line and preparing to leave Nashville if things didn't work out. He wanted someone to be completely honest and to tell him the truth about the quality of his music, and he really wanted the truth, not false encouragement that would lead him to waste more of his time. I have never met Toby Keith, but I must say that I like his style and his uncompromising attitude. He has shown us many times what it takes to man-up, and he isn't afraid to show it; and for that, I respect him as a performer and as a role model to others. He also doesn't take any shit from the media either, and everyone knows that. They have tried, and they remember exactly what happened when they did.

Case in point: Peter Jennings' unflattering comments about a Fourth of July celebration and the supposedly offensive meaning of Toby's song "Courtesy of the Red, White and Blue." Jennings decided to ban the song's lyrics for the celebration.

Toby's response to his comments was, "He's from Canada, isn't he?", thus totally discrediting and beating the journalist at his own game...by informing all of America that he wasn't one of us anyway. A classic boot in the ass resolution!

And then, there was the attack on this goliath of a man by a bunch of liberal little girl country singers who had previously made some extremely political and derogatory remarks about President George W Bush to an unresponsive foreign audience. It turned into a rapid downward spiral immediately for them, as soon as American country music fans had heard what they had said. Challenging Toby was yet another costly mistake that turned most of America against them, and was basically the beginning of the end of the Dixie Chicks; the near-total destruction of their entire careers was the result.

Anyway, this record executive punches in Toby's demo tape and listens to about 20 seconds of the first song, then he fast-forwards to the next and the next and then the next. Finally, he pops the tape out and flips it into Toby's hands, and he smirks, shakes his head in a disapproving manner, and says, "Well, I guess that you're an all right singer and all, but your songwriting and all of your songs are terrible and I can't use you."

Now, this is really interesting to me, because Toby was really grateful that someone whom he thought was an expert had told him the truth. So Toby actually thanked the guy and left. Thank God for placing the correct people in their natural order, because soon after, Toby did leave Nashville and returned to Oklahoma. But divine intervention was soon to intervene, in the form of a fan on an airplane that would change everything.

Toby's very same demo tape was given to another producer (one that actually knew real talent) and the rest is history. The same songs went on to sell millions of records, and the title song, "Should Have Been a Cowboy", was later the most-played song of the entire decade.

It is mind numbing to think how another person could be so overwhelmingly incompetent and monumentally stupid without being labeled as severely mentally handicapped. The interesting fact is that I witnessed Toby Keith telling this very same story, and as he did, he described the same events, except that this time, Toby recalled it while, at the same time, his picture was on the cover of People magazine, and the know-it-all record honcho, Mr. Buzz, was completely out of the business.

It's not surprising; he clearly didn't know what the hell he was doing. He was placed in a position that was out of sync for him, and he simply could not deliver...nor did he have the knowledge and vision for what he was asked to do. Has this type of incompetence ever happened to you? I would wager that it has...probably many times.

That, my friend, is what this section and its message are all about. It seems that there are mysterious forces that are taking over and trying, oftentimes succeeding, at changing the Natural Order of things, and manipulating the outcome for their own agenda.

How is this being done? Easy: the media is often the terminal from which all of this is being played to you, through TV movies and all other streams of communication.

The persons that are responsible think differently than we do, and are projecting their ideas and observations onto us using these weapons, and it is a very powerful and cunning plan of deception. They think that you, as a viewer, can be fooled, and will follow along if they can make it seem as though their message looks more attractive, is easier and is a better way to live your life.

It makes no difference to them whether or not their message is going to cause irreparable harm, possibly destroying our current civilization as we know it. History means nothing to these people, and they think that you are too stupid to make an educated decision for yourself. They think that the collective or the government should do your thinking for you.

The founding fathers, who wrote the greatest and most sophisticated documents in history, knew what big government was capable of doing and they tried to make sure that this would not happen to this country.

And they were willing to fight and die if necessary for this belief. And fight and die, they did. The American Revolution was basically started because of unfair taxes and the desire for freedom from tyranny.

Today, in modern times, we are being faced with the same type of aggression through the liberal media. They are using any and all means necessary to defeat you and I, by using lies and tricks to fool us into thinking their way.

Here is the problem that they face, though: their plan will not work. People are different, we are not all the same. Individuality and self-expression are forever implanted in all of us. We are not all the same. On a spiritual level, and I believe this to be true, we all are somehow connected to each other, but as a whole, all human beings are created equal but different. We are each unique and special, with our own thoughts and ideas.

Hollywood has been trying desperately to change the way we think and act by using their creative abilities, and methods of mind control and visual manipulation. A good example would be the movie **Brokeback Mountain,** a homosexual love story between two cowboys that was publicized and paraded across America as being a film of extreme importance. Its message was of how true love and compassion would conquer all, and its approval by all of America and its rightful place in society, was welcomed and accepted. We were told that the film was an inspiring and compelling love story that was being enjoyed by everyone across America.

However, that was not the truth. There were heated debates and scores of people across the country that were disgusted and really pissed off, particularly by the fact that Hollywood was lying about the overall acceptance of the film by the general public.

The commercials were saying, **"Brokeback Mountain** has won all of America's hearts." Wow! is that what really was happening? Was this movie of such monumental, lasting importance to the American people? To Hollywood, it was, I can assure you. Knowing full well, ahead of time, that this sensitive subject was not going to be accepted by mainstream Americans.

Me personally, I believe in love and that it is a person's own choice to make up their own mind as to whoever and whatever makes them happy. It is none of my business, as long as it doesn't affect me or my life in a harmful manner. Gay people should have all of the same rights as everyone else as far as I am concerned, but marriage is a sacred bond that should be between a man and a woman.

However, I am concerned by the fact that they were trying to deceive and distort its message and views to the public, by pre-selling its overwhelming public approval and acceptance behind the guise of the media's advertising to the masses. It wasn't a successful movie as far as profits were concerned, and by Hollywood's own prime requirement for success, it failed miserably and was a big loser by all the usual Hollywood standards.

However, it still got nominated for the most prestigious and important award possible: the **Academy Award for the Best Picture of the Year.**

I find that Hollywood seems to play whatever side it wishes, and very often misses the mark. They aren't making a very good product, it appears, these days and are always copying each other with more and more of the same types of films.

I compared the movie **Cadillac Records** to this and other films and was confused as to why this movie wasn't up for the Best Picture award, why the actors who portrayed such important real life events had little-to-none of the same admiration from Hollywood executives.

It was a very good movie, yet it received zilch as far as approval from Hollywood. All of the actors were uncommonly good, and all of them should have been nominated for and received more acclaim for their work. See it, if you haven't; it really is a remarkable film. Then watch **Brokeback Mountain** and you decide for yourself which was the better film. Don't just take my word for it.

Television is also trying to change the Natural Order of things. Men are constantly being broken down, by telling everyone that they have somehow acted inappropriately by simply being themselves. Perhaps their conduct isn't exactly proper, but all men should aspire to be themselves and to follow their own paths.

Recently, football legend and Super Bowl winning quarterback Joe Namath was chastised for appearing to be drunk in an interview with an ESPN female reporter named Bonnie. He was obviously feeing no pain, and was looking like he was having a good time during the interview.

He was flirting with the reporter and merely said, "I think I want to kiss you!" I was baffled and shocked that, instead of being flattered by Broadway Joe's advances, she was somehow offended by his comments. I was even more surprised that she didn't actually grab Joe around the neck, and plant one on him. I mean, let's all tell the truth here, it's Joe Namath. Hell, I would have kissed him!

It's also very contradictory behavior, because I have seen this same reporter in the men's locker room, and it didn't seem to bother her when there were completely naked men walking around. And this guy is a legendary super-stud, who was so good looking, confident, and charismatic that he appeared in television commercials while wearing panty hose.

Once, while injured from playing, he watched the game from the sideline wearing a fur coat and sunglasses. He was also a successful movie star and one of the greatest football heroes America has ever seen. But, more importantly, and this was the stone cold fact, is that Joe Namath had been the desire of millions of women for the past 40 years, and she wasn't exactly Ann- Margret in her prime. He was just flirting, and one would think that she would have been smitten.

But, wait! It's the media police! We can't have this famous former lady killer of the past trying to exhibit his "Natural Order" male qualities and desires for a woman while he's drunk on TV. Our young males might actually see what a man does if he wants to playfully ask a woman for a smooch! They might figure out that not all men are namby-pamby weaklings.

Quick, before it's too late, let's attack! And for what? Joe was being a man, a man who was basically being his true self, and by God, he wanted a kiss! It's not like he attacked her for a kiss, or asked her for sex on national TV or embarrassed her. He only wanted to kiss her. What is so terribly wrong with such an action, that it would require and demand an apology, so as not to lose his sponsors and possibly his very livelihood? Any other woman, including my own mother, would have chased Joe through the studio with a bottle of scotch and called for a commercial break.

Thank God that it wasn't me up there on that show, because I actually met my wife of twenty-two years by actually biting her on the ass in a bar the very first time I ever saw her. At the time, I didn't even know her name. But just like Joe, I knew I wanted a bite of that exquisite bottom, so I did! Unfortunately, I have had a bad taste in my mouth ever since! (Sorry, baby, I know that joke is getting old.)

Anyway, if I had done such a thing today, I would be accused of and arrested for sexual harassment and castrated in public. Jesus, I would have to give an apology, written in my own blood, to satisfy the media. Good thing my wife liked it. Because if she hadn't, none of our beautiful children would ever have been born.

Joe did apologize, which was barely sincere, and the event was quickly forgotten, but still, it exemplifies the media's hunger for changing men as they see fit.

It really makes you see things a bit more clearly when you think about how the Natural Order affects man. I can see the men who are correctly placed, and see the ones that are not.

Did you ever see the **Seinfeld** show, when he was coerced into wearing the ruffled pirate shirt? When he walked out of the dressing room wearing this puffy sleeved shirt, with that pitiful and disgusted look on his face, he was hysterically funny. He knew that he looked absolutely ridiculous. And he did, and it was so funny. Obviously, it was not right.

However, Tom Jones wore the very same type of shirt, and he looked great and more than likely still does. Why? Because he can, and it is supposed to be that way. It just looks right. Even if Seinfeld was an entertainer of Tom Jones's type, he still would have looked silly. "The Natural Order is effortless calm harmony with yourself, who you are , what you are doing, and what you should or shouldn't be doing. It is the perfect alignment of all things in the universe, the way it should be. It just feels right and isn't something that can be manufactured. "

It's Elvis Presley in his finest hour, wearing black leather in his 1968 Comeback special, absolutely destroying the audience and seeing the looks on women's faces as he walked out and reclaimed his crown as the King of rock and roll.

It's Jimi Hendrix on stage at Woodstock in front of a half a million people playing the Star Spangled Banner solo at dawn.

It's Michael Jackson singing "Billie Jean" and moon-walking on the Motown Special, to a mesmerized audience who had never before seen such genius.

Or the late Johnny Cash and how the timbre of his voice resonated through the radio like a locomotive humming down the tracks, singing "Burning Ring of Fire".

It's Burt Reynolds in his natural prime, as he stares into the camera, winks and gives us the instant smile that so naturally comes to his face.

It's watching film of Barry Sanders breaking through the line, seeing the whites of his eyes wide open, as he takes a hand-off and then seems to actually sense tacklers long before they can ever get him.

It's Michael Jordan in slow motion, defying gravity and soaring through the air, taking flight and slam-dunking the basketball with incredible force.

It's Muhammad Ali in the exact moment that he proclaims to the world that he is the greatest, dancing in the ring with such effortless grace and ease.

It's Albert Einstein's letter that written to President Roosevelt, imploring him to be careful of the devastating possibilities of the atomic bomb if it were to be placed in the wrong hands, before it was known to be possible and had ever been created.

It's Michelangelo, lying on his back for four years, 68 feet in the air as he paints one of his most celebrated masterpieces: the Sistine Chapel.

Or legendary Las Vegas entertainer Tommy Rocker as he performs on stage by himself, armed only with an old guitar, a drum machine, and talent. Defying all the skeptics who all said it couldn't be done, as he makes plans to open his fourth Vegas casino bar!

It's the sincerity and resolve in Winston Churchill's voice, and the inspiring life or death message which he delivers, so passionately, in his most famous speech: "We shall never surrender!"

It's the confidence in John F. Kennedy's ability to look directly thought the lens of the camera, and his uncanny ability to be almost able to touch you.

It is in the painting of George Washington crossing the Delaware on Christmas in the freezing, dead cold of winter, for the victory that would soon give birth to America .

Or the incredible blind Italian tenor Andrea Bocelli as he hit's the completely out of reach high note and then smashes it with such ease and perfection.

Its Benjamin Franklin flying a kite in a lightning and thunderstorm while his mind contemplates the infinite possibilities and discoveries that await him.

Finally, it is Jesus of Nazareth, with his most beautiful purity, as the bloodied spikes of iron were being nailed, bludgeoned into his hands and feet as he was hung upon the cross. His steadfast, loving, unwavering commitment and the belief in his purity and his love of all God's children. His supreme supernatural strength, power and refusal to ever be broken, to lie or to ask his father, God Almighty, for mercy or revenge. As he exclaims, "Forgive them, Father, for they know not what they do."

He remained steadfast and dying for the sins of man. He is the ultimate man, who showed the entire world his unfailing and highest devotion to all other men and his homage for the supreme glory of man. His sacrifice is the only example that there is no equal in the history for in the entire universe, and of all living things ever known. He manned-up!

I am asking you to look, search your heart, for the same things and to find your place in the Natural Order of life, to become a man who can show the world you are proud and confident of who you really are; that you are not to be fooled or tricked into being someone that you are not and do not have to be. You can be a man and still be gentle, kind and good, but you also have that ability and power to rise to any occasion. To be among your brethren of the greatest men of all time, and to know that they are all your brothers and that their greatness and accomplishments are also a part of each and everyone of us. And you must man-up, because we need you now more than ever. You must take your stand and find your place in the "Natural Order."

Judge of your natural character by what you do in your dreams.

Ralph Waldo Emerson

CHAPTER 10:

FINAL THOUGHTS

Well, there will certainly never be a problem with stories and conversation ideas for my next project, because the world as we know it is constantly changing. Men are still going to be men and we will have to face all of these challenges with a firm stance.

However; I am very concerned with the ongoing monumental problem issues…such as poverty, illegal immigration, health care, inflation, wars, and violent crime in America. Lately it seems that the criminals who commit these senseless acts of violence seem to be getting more egregious and heinous every day. And something has to be done or we are all in danger of being a victim and talking about it is not the answer. It is time to act.

Case in point: the terrible mass shooting that has just occurred in Tucson, Arizona. This mentally disturbed person was already known to be very unstable and had already shown his violent behavior, and he should have been identified and stopped before it happened.

This is another case which should finally convince others who demand political correctness and want more gun control that the people, who are a real threat and that are a danger to law abiding citizens, are the criminals, and, it is the criminals that have the guns. Why? Because there is rarely anyone ever there to stop them, and there is little deterrent.

It sickens me to see the mug shot photograph of the killer's wild eyes and his shaved bald head as he is seen, eerily menacing and peering into the camera, with a look of joyfulness and satisfaction across his smiling face. I cannot stop thinking about the poor victims and their families and all of their loved ones who have to endure such loss and pain. I pray that one day we will be able to take monsters and other ilk like him and be able to completely remove their defective genes from our entire gene pool forever.

His mental illness, or mental disorder, is absolutely no excuse as far as I am concerned. You can argue that point until the sun no longer shines, because, regardless of why, the bottom line is that he did it. He carefully planned it and it was premeditated, and now all of those innocent people are all dead.

Is medication and the need for more treatment your argument and is that what he needed, would medicine have stopped it? Determined killers always find a way.

I also don't care for, and have very deep suspicions about, all of the so-called professional doctors or psychologists that seem to know it all and that have all the exact, right, and correct answers for his mental state and exact reasons why that this person committed this crime. They can magically analyze and instantly diagnose all of his symptoms in a mater of minutes and their findings are, many times, taken as gospel. Most of the time not one of these college educated primo-donnas has the balls or the gut's to say what everyone watching already knows.

That this crazy bastard is a sinister murdering monster who is a danger to everyone and should be destroyed for what he did. I could have told you in two seconds…as soon as I saw him walking and his weird appearance, and had seen him talking to himself and his bizarre behavior, and I don't need to have a medical license. But then again, I also don't give a damn about the possibility of being in violation of being politically correct when it comes to the protection of my wife and our children's lives.

Hurting someone else's feelings…if I am caught cautiously staring at another person who appears to look like they are dangerous and crazy is of absolutely no importance to me. To not do so would be wrong. I am always on the look-out for such people and always am aware of my surroundings at all times. My father and my mentors have all taught me to constantly be on the look out, and I am….and you should be too.

Unfortunately, we will never really know why the shooter in Tucson really committed these crimes and the truth is that no one knows for absolute sure why he did it…there are only opinions and guesses about whether or not he is really completely or even partially mentally ill. I do not know if he is insane or not…I think that he is just evil and it has always been lurking in his soul, and his mind is that of a diabolical killer.

Was Adolph Hitler insane? He ordered, was responsible for, and gruesomely killed millions of innocent people, and a hell of a lot of more people than this guy did, and most historians tend to agree with his usual portrayal as being a monstrously demonic representation of evil, and that he was not mentally ill. How do you decide? Does your resume determine such things as being empirically correct?

Do you believe that there is evil in the world? And if you do (which obviously there is and always has been), would you agree? Or do you think that we accept medical illness as the truth and should incarcerate and continue to allow these instruments of evil to exist and try to cure all of them? If you don't agree that there are indeed evil people in the world and forces of evil, then you are already dead...or perhaps could soon be because of your opinions.

Because no one will ever survive, if you are the target of such a thing and you are not willing to take the necessary steps to defend and save yourself, your family, or your country, regardless of the reason why.

If everyone there was also armed and possessed the will and the training to properly have dispensed with this maniac at the very moment he was first seen with his deadly intent or was preparing to shoot, then most if not all of these innocent people, including that precious 9 year old little girl might have survived.

I know that you have heard this many times before but..."Guns do not kill people...people do!" And blaming the guns and their owners is not the answer to the problem and it is not truthful, either.

Do you blame your pencil when you misspell a word? Of course not, and it is the exact same thing. I do agree, however; that properly identifying gun buyers and owners is sensible and reasonable. Known criminals, mental patients, and felons who have been properly identified should be restricted, but it still won't completely work, and is not a complete deterrent. It will not be 100 percent effective.

The only way to stop these kinds of tragic events from ever occurring, or at the very least, to help citizens stop and give us a fair chance against these kind of sneak attacks…is by adhering to the tried and true method of the past. When people had to fend for themselves, and all good men, and often women, too, relied on protecting themselves. Why did they do it? Because they had to if they wanted to live. Has it come to that? Ask yourself….I already know.

I wish that there was another viable way. If you know of a sure-fire method that does not consist of an impossible, ineffective plan of disarming the entire country, and you have the answer that can stop these mass-killers from accomplishing their missions of determined hatred and their murderous rampages, in our children's schools, in our homes and in our streets, against all of us…then please contact me immediately, and we will shout it from the rooftops, and we will tell the entire world together! Because the time has come to act and stop this by using whatever means necessary to save ourselves.

It is the adherences and forced rules of "Political Correctness" and the ridiculous rules of having to constantly be carefully watching and guarding our actions, thoughts and words to others that could possibly be the suspects of such behavior that is causing the American people to suffer. And why is it wrong to do so?

Because identifying or profiling the obvious possible perpetrators (such as the shooter in Tucson) might offend the ones who are innocent. So we all must continue to body search little old ladies with walkers at the airports and totally ignore Middle-Eastern-looking men who suspiciously look or act exactly like the majority of terrorists, who for the past 50 years have carried out death and destruction at will.

Our enemies are all laughing at us…and they are counting on our own laws and their allies, the "Political Correctness" enforcers, to aid them in the destruction of America. And they are right, because we cannot even completely stop our own people from continuously making up new political correctness bullshit and expecting us to obey.

Whatever happened to society's rights and to the people's rights who disagree with Political Correctness, and all of those people who want to survive? Why aren't we the ones inventing new and magical words to describe our own agenda, for our kind of correct, social sensitivity awareness…only in reverse? You know, a better, super-cool, catchy word that will actually save peoples lives.

Now there's an idea! Hey, how about this: from this moment on, why don't all men right now reach one hand down into their pants and check to see if they still have their balls intact? And then we can all start acting like real men should act and stop being afraid of being politically correct, and focus all of our determination, strength and resolve on actually trying to save America and all of its citizens from death and total annihilation! And then let's proudly call it "**Honest and Truth Correctness**!" And let's see if it catches on and how well it works.

One day, when citizens can no longer tolerate it, the necessary change will appear. It always has before. I believe that is how it has always been throughout the ages and always will be. It is very depressing, sad, and ultimately tragic to know what our history and our past methods for resolution have been, and what it will inevitably be again when it arrives. But the result is survival and ultimately peace.

It seems amazing to me, that there are now allegations against **Sarah Palin** and the notion that she is somehow bizarrely responsible for this shooting. Apparently, it is all because of a comment or something she has had posted on her web site that could have quite possibly have motivated this monster into going berserk! It is insanely preposterous and irresponsible to even remotely connect her and try to tie her name to this massacre.

Obviously the persons responsible for this journalistic character sabotage has another agenda in mind and is trying to besmirch her image and name.

I am not surprised, though; the same persons that are responsible for this kind of journalism, of a convoluted and contrived pack of lies, are also responsible for spending countless days, hours, and ultimately years covering other real important and immensely historic life changing events...such as the non-stop train wreck lives of Anna Nichole Smith, Lindsay Lohan and now, most recently, Snooki, and the immense importance of their drunken exploits and debauchery, and why all young girls should be just like them. Yuck!

The reason for this attempt of journalistic carnage against Sarah Palin, and now even Sharon Angle of Nevada has also been mentioned, is very clear, and it can be recognized immediately, and that is fear. They fear these women with the utmost intensity, and they are willing to do anything to try and stop them. Even if it means describing and concocting the most ridiculously far-fetched whale's tail of a bunch of lies as humanly possible.

The media has had lots of practice and are very skilled at crafting their web of deception, which is also why they fail. You cannot fool all of the American people and not everyone is as stupid as they think. And that is one of their main strategies: that most Americans are just too stupid to take care of themselves and that the government should take care of everyone. Mainly by punishing the little guy, the successful small business, hard-working person who pays taxes, creates jobs and has actually tried to create something and to live the American Dream, and then reward the people who don't. Does this make any sense?

I guess it does if you are trying to convert everyone into becoming slaves of the government and label everyone as the same, into becoming socialists. Several members of the far-left liberal media are reporting that Sarah Palin's political career is in grave danger and is over. Wow…have these people been drug tested? Are they all on crack? What in the hell is going on? Quick, attention! Someone please call the media police immediately, because there must be a new and improved super-crack that has made it into the country. But beware, because it causes severe permanent brain damage and apparently only affects liberal journalists. It's very easy to spot: they all appear very confused and incredibly stupid!

We shall see if her career is really over and time will tell, however, I personally think she is going to be around for as long as she wishes to be and she has only recently begun to experience her success. She could quite possibly be the first woman President of the United States of America and this feeble attempt will prove to be of little importance if she chooses to run.

Recently, I saw a special report on Neil Cavuto's show on **Fox News** television. Neil noticed the obvious trend by some of the media, which is that men and our true images are being attacked. He noticed that this is rampantly happening and his story was very poignant and straight to the point. Neil's style is very easy to understand, and I like his commentary. I also really enjoy Sean Hannity, Glenn Beck and of course Bill O'Reilly.

They impress me because they are constantly manning-up and it's great to see them do so. Those guys really like to scrap and mix it up, and I think they are all role models and are making a difference. I don't always agree with everything that they say, but most of the time they are dead on. Maybe that can explain why Fox News is number one. Their ratings consistently beat out all of the major networks and surpass all of the competition...combined. I also have noticed how much fun they seem to have. They all, for the most part, are usually smiling and are at ease They all appear relaxed and are very poised.

Occasionally I will watch **MSNBC** with Keith Olbermann, usually just to get his reaction from something that one of the Fox boys has said that is sure to absolutely infuriate him...and he never ceases to disappoint! He is always so mad and disgruntled. I find his tantrums very funny, and I really enjoy his general disgust with all things associated with the Right. I am amazed at how easy it is to completely control him and get him to react to their obvious enticement. Maybe he is doing it on purpose to try and boost his ratings, (which are minute in comparison) because I don't see anyone else flipping out so easily and on a regular basis. His constantly scowling face says it all; check it out for yourself...you too will see the difference.

Rush Limbaugh is also very entertaining and he is also from Missouri, which automatically qualifies him. I am a registered Republican...(just like one of my heroes, Abraham Lincoln) However, I also have many fundamental Democratic beliefs and am actually an Independent, who always votes his conscience. Many of my beliefs are ultra-conservative, liberal and are extreme, but I believe that sometimes you must fight fire with fire, especially when your survival is at stake. My soul and conscience wish that this was not the required method of resolution.

I also firmly believe in the power of love. Another thing about me is that I cherish America and everything that it stands for and I am against anyone or anything that threatens her. I would be more than willing to defend this country, our way of life and all of our people to the death or whatever that situation requires, to save her.

A few months ago when Bill O'Reilly was on **The View** and Whoopi Goldberg and Joy Behar both got up and stormed out under protest, I couldn't stop laughing at them and their silly protest attempt. Here are, supposedly, two professional women celebrities who are engaged in expressing and dispensing their own widely known liberal agenda and leftist opinions to millions of viewers and who are both constantly preaching and exercising their 1st amendment rights of free speech, and the instant that someone else has a different opinion and has something to say that they don't agree with, they completely lose their minds! It was funny and it still is, because of the irony and contradictions of their own actions.

Note: to the girls: next time, if you are going to challenge Bill O'Reilly to an intellectual street fight, you'd better think twice about it and be sure to bring your "A-game" with you, because you were both terribly exposed, to all of America (especially the show's leader and main producer Barbara Walters), as being incredibly unprofessional. You both were "taken to school" and only ended up humiliating and embarrassing yourselves by your own hypocritical actions.

More important than this obvious besting, and the verbal and mental defeat of these two women, were Bill's actual comments which were 100 percent correct: that "We were attacked by Muslim terrorists on 9-11." And any one who disagrees with this assessment of this historical, tragic, and supremely cowardly event, is either a complete idiot or is not an American. There is no room, in my opinion, for the mincing of words in regard to being sensitive to the feelings of the Muslim terrorists who did this to our country...who sneak attacked and killed our people. "F-them all straight to Hell!" is what I say.....and God bless America!

I have deep and sincere admiration for all of the firemen and police who protect all of us and who put their lives on the line every day. They are all heroes as far as I am concerned. Death is a real possibility for these brave Americans everyday they go to work. I have had the privilege of meeting and becoming friends with several firefighters and police officers while living here in Las Vegas, and I have known many others from back home in Kansas City as well. They all seem to have a special quality about them; they face real and present danger every day and we should all respect their commitment and acknowledge their service.

Recently retired and legendary firefighter, Harold Wyatt of Las Vegas in particular is a man whom I deeply admire and I consider him a stellar role model and mentor. He is mentally and physically rock-solid and he speaks with a powerful and bold directness. He leads by example. His fellow Vegas firefighters respect him immensely and his humility is exceptional. He is also feared, and I know why, he doesn't take any shit from anyone, but he still commands his common sense and wisdom. And I respect him very much. He exlimplifies this book.

Our military is the greatest fighting force in the world and all of those brave and courageous men and women deserve our admiration and wholehearted confidence and respect. And God bless all of our veterans as well...especially our combat veterans who have all sacrificed and given so much for our country. There are no words that can truly ever repay you for what you have all done for each and every one of us.

And finally....every other person, man woman and child in this country that contributes and has given to the betterment and well being of the nation, we wholeheartedly salute you and are proud and grateful for your sustaining contribution. The American workforce in the past has had no equal, and I believe that we might have stumbled but we have not yet fallen. Our history and our struggle have shown exactly what kind of amazing feats we are capable of and why we simply cannot ever be defeated when we combine our strength and determined effort for any situation or calling. America stands for liberty and freedom.

It is our signature motto, and we boldly serve as a shinning example of this to the entire rest of the world. I have little regard or respect for countries such as France who, often smugly, dare to criticize us and seem to look down upon our actions in such a condescending manner and tone. There are countless cemeteries all over Europe filled with fallen American hero's.

Those countries that do so all owe us an overwhelming, immense debt that was bought and paid for with American blood and the sacrifice of hundreds of thousands of our soldiers lives…twice! To my knowledge, this has never been duplicated in world history. One would think that all who would do so would be more grateful, and realize the sacrifice we have made for them, because without America many other nations (especially France) in the world and their entire civilization and culture would have been completely destroyed, or would have been enslaved and/or starved to death., without America having saved their asses.

We must continue doing all of the things that have made us so great, if we are to sustain our country, our families, and our way of life. We cannot do so if we continue to make it possible for ourselves to sabotage and implode our country from within. Political Correctness is making it possible for our enemies' to destroy us from within, by using our own laws against us and they must be stopped.

"America will never be destroyed from the outside. If we falter and lose our freedoms, it will be because we destroyed ourselves."   *Abraham Lincoln*

Rome, and many other civilizations, were also destroyed by this historical systematic method of self-destruction. If you don't believe me, then look it up for yourself, it is all written in the history books. Political correctness, the general lack of wisdom and common sense, and the fear of reprisal of speaking up against these poisonous vipers, are often the culprits, and it is imminent danger for all of us…but they are growing and getting stronger every day.

As men, we have a duty and responsibility to stop them all from destroying us. We must continue to be the instruments that we were intended to be and that our creator that has designed us into, our natural form. It is our timeless and true natural order as men. The seemingly correct way it has always been, since the dawn of time, and doing the things we always have had to do in order to survive.

Men, our image is being attacked, and it is now up to you to decide for yourself if I am right or not. I believe that I have shown you, in vivid detail, and now you must decide and proclaim to yourself as well, by agreeing and acknowledging that the necessary methods for manning-up are as follows:

1. Reason
2. Take action.
3. Responsibility
4. Conviction, Passion
5. Do it on your own terms.
6. Common sense and Wisdom
7. Be the example
8. Mentor
9. The Natural Order

And if you agree, then this has been a complete victory for all. And those who now agree and righteously proclaim it to be so, are now ready to solemnly swear and do hereby pledge this oath:

"THE MAN UP OATH"

I am a man.
I must take action whenever needed.
I willingly accept all responsibility, on my own terms.
I do so with passion and conviction.
I always fully exercise wisdom and common sense.
I am the example to others.
I am a mentor.
I rightfully take my place in the natural order.

Date_____

Sign_____

Congratulations! You have now officially succeeded and have passed the written portion of the test and are now ready to "Man-Up", and are now hereby recognized to use your new abilities and prowess at will and to help all others to find themselves and to become masters in their own right. To Man-Up as required......

"Do you want to know who you are? Don't ask. Act! Action will delineate and define you."

Thomas Jefferson

Be bold and boast, just like the cock beside the hen.

Aeschylus

This has been a lot of fun, and I am excited to get this information out to anyone who is interested. I have really enjoyed writing this book and I hope you too will enjoy reading it and that you will realize that I'm not joking and that there is a real problem that needs to be addressed. I have tried to make it entertaining, and fast and easy reading for you, and it isn't meant to be a high thought process kind of message. It is my simple and direct attempt to show real examples of what is all around us and the consequences if we continue on this path.

We are planning on taking "The Official Man-Up Show" (www.theofficialmanupshow.com) to the air-waves as soon as possible and I originally wrote the show for television, but we will broadcast live on the web and from radio as soon as we can and we will also stream all previous shows from our web site.

You can also reach me through my personal web site, www.michaelparrish.com and e-mail me your questions and or comments. And I hope that you will watch and listen because the show is intended to be a lot of fun and it will also be entertaining and informative. We have big plans and are thinking of new and unique ideas to do on the show. Please contact us at the web site for any ideas you might have because that is what we want to do with all of our listeners. We also have planned to continue to spread the man-up word and hope you will too.

We are planning to have a kind of "Man-Up-a-Pallooza" here in Vegas, and possibly feature and host other man-up events around the county. We would love to bring the "The Official Man Up Show" to Kansas City and to see all of our home town fans! Everything we are planning will be available through our web site and it will also be our main contact point.

That's pretty much how the show is going to look and what the content will be; however, the show is really about having fun and is meant to be entertaining and still get our important message across. So I am sure that we will be trying new and different ideas. Also, I am planning on inviting a lot of famous special guests and celebrities to appear on the show and express their views and opinions. Stimulating debate and good conversation is our intension so let us know who you would like us to have on the show and we will do our best to get them on.

Ask yourself this...one simple question, who doesn't or wouldn't want to join us and man-up? To take action, accept responsibility, show others how and to mentor our fellow Americans and make a stand against injustice for the greater good? Well, now you know, and its up to all of us to stay focused and be prepared to..."Burn the ship's"

Thanks again, and God Bless... and don't ever be afraid to "Man-Up!"

"A nation or civilization that continues to produce soft-minded men purchases its own spiritual death on the installment plan."

Martin Luther King. Jr.

"A strong body makes the mind strong. As to the species of exercises, I advise the gun. While this gives moderate exercise to the body, it gives boldness, enterprise and independence to the mind. Games played with the ball, and others of that nature, are too violent for the body and stamp no character on the mind. Let your gun therefore be your constant companion of your walks."

Thomas Jefferson

www.ingramcontent.com/pod-product-compliance
Lightning Source LLC
Chambersburg PA
CBHW060929040426
42445CB00011B/852